COLLECTED POEMS OF Æ

COLLECTED POEMS OF Æ

WILDSIDE PRESS

COLLECTED POEMS OF Æ

Published in 2008 by Wildside Press.
www.wildsidepress.com

CONTENTS

EPIGRAM

OH, be not led away,
Lured by the colour of the sun-rich day.
　The gay romance of song
Unto the spirit life doth not belong:
　Though far-between the hours
In which the Master of Angelic powers
　Lightens the dusk within
The holy of holies, be it thine to win
　Rare vistas of white light,
Half-parted lips through which the Infinite
　Murmurs its ancient story,
Hearkening to whom the wandering planets hoary
　Waken primeval fires,
With deeper rapture in celestial choirs
　Breathe, and with fleeter motion
Wheel in their orbits through the surgeless ocean.
　So hearken thou like these,
Intent on it, mounting by slow degrees,
　Until thy song's elation
Echoes the multitudinous meditation.

AWAKENING

THE LIGHTS shone down the street
In the long blue close of day:
A boy's heart beat sweet, sweet,
As it flowered in its dreamy clay.

Beyond the dazzling throng
And above the towers of men
The stars made him long, long,
To return to their light again.

They lit the wondrous years
And his heart within was gay;
But a life of tears, tears,
He had won for himself that day.

BY THE MARGIN OF
THE GREAT DEEP

WHEN the breath of twilight blows to flame the misty skies,
All its vaporous sapphire, violet glow and silver gleam
With their magic flood me through the gateway of the eyes;
   I am one with the twilight's dream.

When the trees and skies and fields are one in dusky mood,
Every heart of man is rapt within the mother's breast:
Full of peace and sleep and dreams in the vasty quietude,
   I am one with their hearts at rest.

From our immemorial joys of hearth and home and love
Strayed away along the margin of the unknown tide,
All its reach of soundless calm can thrill me far above
   Word or touch from the lips beside.

Aye, and deep and deep and deeper let me drink and draw
From the olden fountain more than light or peace or dream,
Such primeval being as o'erfills the heart with awe,
   Growing one with its silent stream.

THE UNKNOWN GOD

FAR up the dim twilight fluttered
  Moth-wings of vapour and flame:
The lights danced over the mountains,
  Star after star they came.

The lights grew thicker unheeded,
  For silent and still were we;
Our hearts were drunk with a beauty
  Our eyes could never see.

THE HERMIT

NOW the quietude of earth
Nestles deep my heart within;
Friendships new and strange have birth
Since I left the city's din.

Here the tempest stays its guile,
Like a big kind brother plays,
Romps and pauses here awhile
From its immemorial ways.

Now the silver light of dawn,
Slipping through the leaves that fleck
My one window, hurries on,
Throws its arms around my neck.

Darkness to my doorway hies,
Lays her chin upon the roof,
And her burning seraph eyes
Now no longer keep aloof.

And the ancient mystery
Holds its hands out day by day,
Takes a chair and croons with me
By my cabin built of clay.

When the dusky shadow flits,
By the chimney nook I see
Where the old enchanter sits,
Smiles and waves and beckons me.

OVERSOUL

I am Beauty itself among beautiful things.
—Bhagavad-Gita.

THE EAST was crowned with snow-cold bloom
And hung with veils of pearly fleece:
They died away into the gloom,
Vistas of peace—and deeper peace.

And earth and air and wave and fire
In awe and breathless silence stood;
For One who passed into their choir
Linked them in mystic brotherhood.

Twilight of amethyst, amid
Thy few strange stars that lit the heights,
Where was the secret spirit hid?
Where was Thy place, O Light of Lights?

The flame of Beauty far in space—
Where rose the fire: in Thee? in Me?
Which bowed the elemental race
To adoration silently?

THE GREAT BREATH

ITS edges foamed with amethyst and rose,
Withers once more the old blue flower of day:
There where the ether like a diamond glows
   Its petals fade away.

A shadowy tumult stirs the dusky air;
Sparkle the delicate dews, the distant snows;
The great deep thrills, for through it everywhere
   The breath of Beauty blows.

I saw how all the trembling ages past,
Moulded to her by deep and deeper breath,
Neared to the hour when Beauty breathes her last
   And knows herself in death.

DUSK

DUSK wraps the village in its dim caress;
Each chimney's vapour, like a thin grey rod,
Mounting aloft through miles of quietness,
  Pillars the skies of God.

Far up they break or seem to break their line,
Mingling their nebulous crests that bow and nod
Under the light of those fierce stars that shine
  Out of the calm of God.

Only in clouds and dreams I felt those souls
In the abyss, each fire hid in its clod;
From which in clouds and dreams the spirit rolls
  Into the vast of God.

NIGHT

HEART-HIDDEN from the outer things I rose;
The spirit woke anew in nightly birth
Unto the vastness where forever glows
   The star-soul of the earth.

There all alone in primal ecstasy,
Within her depths where revels never tire,
The olden Beauty shines: each thought of me
   Is veined through with its fire.

And all my thoughts are throngs of living souls;
They breathe in me, heart unto heart allied;
Their joy undimmed, though when the morning tolls
   The planets may divide.

DAWN

STILL as the holy of holies breathes the vast,
Within its crystal depths the stars grow dim;
Fire on the altar of the hills at last
   Burns on the shadowy rim.

Moment that holds all moments; white upon
The verge it trembles; then like mists of flowers
Break from the fairy fountain of the dawn
   The hues of many hours.

Thrown downward from that high companionship
Of dreaming inmost heart with inmost heart,
Into the common daily ways I slip
   My fire from theirs apart.

DAY

IN day from some titanic past it seems
As if a thread divine of memory runs;
Born ere the Mighty One began his dreams,
   Or yet were stars and suns.

But here an iron will has fixed the bars;
Forgetfulness falls on earth's myriad races:
No image of the proud and morning stars
   Looks at us from their faces.

Yet yearning still to reach to those dim heights,
Each dream remembered is a burning-glass,
Where through to darkness from the Light of Lights
   Its rays in splendour pass.

ECHOES

THE MIGHT that shaped itself through storm and stress
In chaos, here is lulled in breathing sweet;
Under the long brown ridge in gentleness
   Its fierce old pulses beat.

Quiet and sad we go at eve; the fire
That woke exultant in an earlier day
Is dead; the memories of old desire
   Only in shadows play.

We liken love to this and that; our thought
The echo of a deeper being seems:
We kiss, because God once for beauty sought
   Within a world of dreams.

STAR TEACHERS

EVEN as a bird sprays many-coloured fires,
The plumes of paradise, the dying light
Rays through the fevered air in misty spires
    That vanish in the heights.

These myriad eyes that look on me are mine;
Wandering beneath them I have found again
The ancient ample moment, the divine,
    The God-root within men.

For this, for this the lights innumerable
As symbols shine that we the true light win:
For every star and every deep they fill
    Are stars and deeps within.

WINTER

A DIAMOND glow of winter o'er the world:
Amid the chilly halo nigh the west
Flickers a phantom violet bloom unfurled
    Dim on the twilight's breast.

Only phantasmal blooms but for an hour,
A transient beauty; then the white stars shine
Chilling the heart: I long for thee to flower,
    O bud of light divine.

But never visible to sense or thought
The flower of Beauty blooms afar withdrawn;
If in our being then we know it not,
    Or, knowing, it is gone.

ANSWER

THE WARMTH of life is quenched with bitter frost;
Upon the lonely road a child limps by
Skirting the frozen pools: our way is lost:
    Our hearts sink utterly.

But from the snow-patched moorland chill and drear,
Lifting our eyes beyond the spirëd height,
With white-fire lips apart the dawn breathes clear
    Its soundless hymn of light.

Out of the vast the voice of one replies
Whose words are clouds and stars and night and day,
When for the light the anguished spirit cries
    Deep in its house of clay.

THE GIFT

I THOUGHT, beloved, to have brought to you
A gift of quietness and ease and peace,
Cooling your brow as with the mystic dew
   Dropping from twilight trees.

Homeward I go not yet; the darkness grows;
Not mine the voice to still with peace divine:
From the first fount the stream of quiet flows
   Through other hearts than mine.

Yet of my night I give to you the stars,
And of my sorrow here the sweetest gains,
And out of hell, beyond its iron bars,
   My scorn of all its pains.

THE DIVINE VISION

THIS mood hath known all beauty, for it sees
O'erwhelmed majesties
In these pale forms, and kingly crowns of gold
On brows no longer bold,
And through the shadowy terrors of their hell
The love for which they fell,
And how desire which cast them in the deep
Called God too from His sleep.
Oh, Pity, only seer, who looking through
A heart melted like dew,
Seest the long perished in the present thus,
For ever dwell in us.
Whatever time thy golden eyelids ope
They travel to a hope;
Not only backward from these low degrees
To starry dynasties,
But, looking far where now the silence owns
And rules from empty thrones,
Thou seest the enchanted hills of heaven burn
For joy at our return.
Thy tender kiss hath memory we are kings
For all our wanderings.
Thy shining eyes already see the after
In hidden light and laughter.

FROLIC

THE CHILDREN were shouting together
And racing along the sands,
A glimmer of dancing shadows,
A dovelike flutter of hands.

The stars were shouting in heaven,
The sun was chasing the moon:
The game was the same as the children's,
They danced to the self-same tune.

The whole of the world was merry,
One joy from the vale to the height,
Where the blue woods of twilight encircled
The lovely lawns of the light.

DESIRE

WITH Thee a moment! Then what dreams have play!
Traditions of eternal toil arise,
Search for the high, austere and lonely way
The Spirit moves in through eternities.
Ah, in the soul what memories arise!

And with what yearning inexpressible,
Rising from long forgetfulness I turn
To Thee, invisible, unrumoured, still:
White for Thy whiteness all desires burn.
Ah, with what longing once again I turn!

THE PLACE OF REST

The soul is its own witness and its own refuge.

UNTO the deep the deep heart goes,
It lays its sadness nigh the breast:
Only the Mighty Mother knows
The wounds that quiver unconfessed.

It seeks a deeper silence still;
It folds itself around with peace,
Where thoughts alike of good or ill
In quietness unfostered cease.

It feels in the unwounding vast
For comfort for its hopes and fears:
The Mighty Mother bows at last;
She listens to her children's tears.

Where the last anguish deepens—there
The fire of beauty smites through pain:
A glory moves amid despair,
The Mother takes her child again.

THE DAWN OF DARKNESS

COME earth's little children pit-pat from their burrows on the hill;
Hangs within the gloom its weary head the shining daffodil.
In the valley underneath us through the fragrance flit along
Over fields and over hedgerows little quivering drops of song.
All adown the pale blue mantle of the mountains far away
Stream the tresses of the twilight flying in the wake of day.
Night comes; soon alone shall fancy follow sadly in her flight
Where the fiery dust of evening, shaken from the feet of light,
Thrusts its monstrous barriers between the pure, the good, the true,
That our weeping eyes may strain for, but shall never after view.
Only yester eve I watched with heart at rest the nebulæ
Looming far within the shadowy shining of the Milky Way;
Finding in the stillness joy and hope for all the sons of men;
Now what silent anguish fills a night more beautiful than then:
For earth's age of pain has come, and all her sister planets weep,
Thinking of her fires of morning passing into dreamless sleep.
In this cycle of great sorrow for the moments that we last
We too shall be linked by weeping to the greatness of her past:
But the coming race shall know not, and the fount of tears shall dry,
And the arid heart of man be arid as the desert sky.
So within my mind the darkness dawned, and round me everywhere
Hope departed with the twilight, leaving only dumb despair.

WAITING

WHEN the dawn comes forth I wonder
Will our sad, sad hearts awaken,
And the grief we laboured under
From the new-in-joy be shaken?

If the night be long in going,
All our souls will fix in sadness;
And the light of morning glowing
Waken in our eyes no gladness.

All unschooled in mirth we will not
Rouse forgotten joys from sleeping;
And the dawn our pain shall still not:
We will gaze on it with weeping.

THE SYMBOL SEDUCES

THERE in her old-world garden smiles
A symbol of the world's desire,
Striving with quaint and lovely wiles
To bind to earth the soul of fire.

And while I sit and listen there,
The robe of Beauty falls away
From universal things to where
Its image dazzles for a day.

Away! the great life calls; I leave
For Beauty, Beauty's rarest flower;
For Truth, the lips that ne'er deceive;
For Love, I leave Love's haunted bower.

REST

ON me to rest, my bird, my bird:
  The swaying branches of my heart
Are blown by every wind toward
  The home whereto their wings depart.

Build not your nest, my bird, on me;
  I know no peace but ever sway:
O lovely bird, be free, be free,
  On the wild music of the day.

But sometimes when your wings would rest,
  And winds are laid on quiet eves:
Come, I will bear you breast to breast,
  And lap you close with loving leaves.

PITY

THE TWINKLING mists of green and gold
Afloat in the abyss of air,
From out the window high and old
   We watched together there.

The monstrous fabric of the town
Lay black below; the cries of pain
Came to our ears from up and down
   The dimly-lighted lane.

Olive, your eyes were turned to me,
Seeking a soul to sympathise:
I wondered what that glow might be,
   Olive, within your eyes.

Into your trembling words there passed
The sorrow that was sighed through you:
Pity, a breath from out the vast,
   From unknown hollows blew.

THE CITY

Full of Zeus the cities: full of Zeus the harbours:
full of Zeus are all the ways of men.

WHAT domination of what darkness dies this hour,
And through what new, rejoicing, winged, ethereal power
O'erthrown, the cells opened, the heart released from fear?
Gay twilight and grave twilight pass. The stars appear
O'er the prodigious, smouldering, dusky, city flare.
The hanging gardens of Babylon were not more fair
Than these blue flickering glades, where childhood in its glee
Re-echoes with fresh voice the heaven-lit ecstasy.
Yon girl whirls like an eastern dervish. Her dance is
No less a god-intoxicated dance than his,
Though all unknowing the arcane fire that lights her feet,
What motions of what starry tribes her limbs repeat.
I, too, firesmitten, cannot linger: I know there lies
Open somewhere this hour a gate to Paradise,
Its blazing battlements with watchers thronged, O where?
I know not, but my flame-winged feet shall lead me there.
O, hurry, hurry, unknown shepherd of desires,
And with thy flock of bright imperishable fires
Pen me within the starry fold, ere the night falls
And I am left alone below immutable walls.
Or am I there already, and is it Paradise
To look on mortal things with an immortal's eyes?
Above the misty brilliance the streets assume
A night-dilated blue magnificence of gloom
Like many-templed Nineveh tower beyond tower;
And I am hurried on in this immortal hour.
Mine eyes beget new majesties: my spirit greets
The trams, the high-built glittering galleons of the streets
That float through twilight rivers from galaxies of light.
Nay, in the Fount of Days they rise, they take their flight,
And wend to the great deep, the Holy Sepulchre.
Those dark misshapen folk to be made lovely there
Hurry with me, not all ignoble as we seem,
Lured by some inexpressible and gorgeous dream.
The earth melts in my blood. The air that I inhale
Is like enchanted wine poured from the Holy Grail.
What was that glimmer then? Was it the flash of wings

As through the blinded mart rode on the King of Kings?
O stay, departing glory, stay with us but a day,
And burning seraphim shall leap from out our clay,
And plumed and crested hosts shall shine where men have been,
Heaven hold no lordlier court than earth at College Green.
Ah, no, the wizardy is over; the magic flame
That might have melted all in beauty fades as it came.
The stars are far and faint and strange. The night draws down.
Exiled from light, forlorn, I walk in Dublin Town.
Yet had I might to lift the veil, the will to dare,
The fiery rushing chariots of the Lord are there,
The whirlwind path, the blazing gates, the trumpets blown,
The halls of heaven, the majesty of throne by throne,
Enraptured faces, hands uplifted, welcome sung
By the thronged gods, tall, golden-coloured, joyful, young.

DUST

I HEARD them in their sadness say,
"The earth rebukes the thought of God;
We are but embers wrapped in clay
A little nobler than the sod."

But I have touched the lips of clay,
Mother, thy rudest sod to me
Is thrilled with fire of hidden day,
And haunted by all mystery.

THE VIRGIN MOTHER

WHO is that goddess to whom men should pray,
But her from whom their hearts have turned away,
Out of whose virgin being they were born,
Whose mother nature they have named with scorn
Calling its holy substance common clay.

Yet from this so despised earth was made
The milky whiteness of those queens who swayed
Their generations with a light caress,
And from some image of whose loveliness
The heart built up high heaven when it prayed.

Lover, your heart, the heart on which it lies,
Your eyes that gaze and those alluring eyes,
Your lips, the lips they kiss, alike had birth
Within that dark divinity of earth,
Within that mother being you despise.

Ah, when I think this earth on which I tread
Hath borne these blossoms of the lovely dead,
And makes the living heart I love to beat,
I look with sudden awe beneath my feet
As you with erring reverence overhead.

DANA

I AM the tender voice calling "Away,"
Whispering between the beatings of the heart,
And inaccessible in dewy eyes
I dwell, and all unkissed on lovely lips,
Lingering between white breasts inviolate,
And fleeting ever from the passionate touch,
I shine afar, till men may not divine
Whether it is the stars or the beloved
They follow with rapt spirit. And I weave
My spells at evening, folding with dim caress,
Aerial arms and twilight dropping hair,
The lonely wanderer by wood or shore,
Till, filled with some deep tenderness, he yields,
Feeling in dreams for the dear mother heart
He knew, ere he forsook the starry way,
And clings there, pillowed far above the smoke
And the dim murmur from the duns of men.
I can enchant the trees and rocks, and fill
The dumb brown lips of earth with mystery,
Make them reveal or hide the god. I breathe
A deeper pity than all love, myself
Mother of all, but without hands to heal:
Too vast and vague, they know me not. But yet,
I am the heartbreak over fallen things,
The sudden gentleness that stays the blow,
And I am in the kiss that foemen give
Pausing in battle, and in the tears that fall
Over the vanquished foe, and in the highest,
Among the Danaan gods, I am the last
Council of mercy in their hearts where they
Mete justice from a thousand starry thrones.

THE EARTH BREATH

FROM the cool and dark-lipped furrows
    Breathes a dim delight
Through the woodland's purple plumage
    To the diamond night.
Aureoles of joy encircle
    Every blade of grass
Where the dew-fed creatures silent
    And enraptured pass.
And the restless ploughman pauses,
    Turns and, wondering,
Deep beneath his rustic habit
    Finds himself a king;
For a fiery moment looking
    With the eyes of God
Over fields a slave at morning
    Bowed him to the sod.
Blind and dense with revelation
    Every moment flies,
And unto the Mighty Mother,
    Gay, eternal, rise
All the hopes we hold, the gladness,
    Dreams of things to be.
One of all thy generations,
    Mother, hails to thee.
Hail, and hail, and hail for ever,
    Though I turn again
From thy joy unto the human
    Vesture of pain.
I, thy child who went forth radiant
    In the golden prime,
Find thee still the mother-hearted
    Through my night in time;
Find in thee the old enchantment
    There behind the veil
Where the gods, my brothers, linger.
    Hail, forever, hail!

ALTER EGO

ALL the morn a spirit gay
Breathes within my heart a rhyme,
'Tis but hide and seek we play
In and out the courts of time.

Fairy lover, when my feet
Through the tangled woodland go,
'Tis thy sunny fingers fleet
Fleck the fire dews to and fro.

In the moonlight grows a smile
Mid its rays of dusty pearl—
'Tis but hide and seek the while,
As some frolic boy and girl.

When I fade into the deep
Some mysterious radiance showers
From the jewel-heart of sleep
Through the veil of darkened hours.

Where the ring of twilight gleams
Round the sanctuary wrought,
Whispers haunt me—in my dreams
We are one yet know it not.

Some for beauty follow long
Flying traces; some there be
Seek thee only for a song:
I to lose myself in thee.

NATURAL MAGIC

WE air tired who follow after
Phantasy and truth that flies:
You with only look and laughter
Stain our hearts with richest dyes.

When you break upon our study
Vanish all our frosty cares;
As the diamond deep grows ruddy,
Filled with morning unawares.

With the stuff that dreams are made of
But an empty house we build:
Glooms we are ourselves afraid of,
By the ancient starlight chilled.

All unwise in thought or duty—
Still our wisdom envies you:
We who lack the living beauty
Half our secret knowledge rue.

Thought nor fear in you nor dreaming
Veil the light with mist about;
Joy, as through a crystal gleaming,
Flashes from the gay heart out.

Pain and penitence forsaking,
Hearts like cloisters dim and grey,
By your laughter lured, awaking
Join with you the dance of day.

CHILDHOOD

HOW I could see through and through you!
So unconscious, tender, kind,
More than ever was known to you
Of the pure ways of your mind.

We who long to rest from strife
Labour sternly as a duty;
But a magic in your life
Charms, unknowing of its beauty.

We are pools whose depths are told;
You are like a mystic fountain,
Issuing ever pure and cold
From the hollows of the mountain.

We are men by anguish taught
To distinguish false from true;
Higher wisdom we have not;
But a joy within guides you.

THREE COUNSELLORS

IT was the fairy of the place,
Moving within a little light,
Who touched with dim and shadowy grace
The conflict at its fever height.

It seemed to whisper "Quietness,"
Then quietly itself was gone:
Yet echoes of its mute caress
Were with me as the years went on.

It was the warrior within
Who called "Awake, prepare for fight:
Yet lose not memory in the din:
Make of thy gentleness thy might:

"Make of thy silence words to shake
The long-enthroned kings of earth:
Make of thy will the force to break
Their towers of wantonness and mirth."

It was the wise all-seeing soul
Who counselled neither war nor peace:
"Only be thou thyself that goal
In which the wars of time shall cease."

SYMBOLISM

NOW when the spirit in us wakes and broods,
Filled with home yearnings, drowsily it flings
From its deep heart high dreams and mystic moods,
Mixed with the memory of the loved earth things:
Clothing the vast with a familiar face;
Reaching its right hand forth to greet the starry race.

Wondrously near and clear the great warm fires
Stare from the blue; so shows the cottage light
To the field labourer whose heart desires
The old folk by the nook, the welcome bright
From the house-wife long parted from at dawn—
So the star villages in God's great depths withdrawn.

Nearer to Thee, not by delusion led,
Though there no house fires burn nor bright eyes gaze:
We rise, but by the symbol charioted,
Through loved things rising up to Love's own ways:
By these the soul unto the vast has wings
And sets the seal celestial on all mortal things.

IMMORTALITY

WE must pass like smoke or live within the spirit's fire;
For we can no more than smoke unto the flame return
If our thought has changed to dream, our will unto desire,
   As smoke we vanish though the fire may burn.

Lights of infinite pity star the grey dusk of our days:
Surely here is soul: with it we have eternal breath:
In the fire of love we live, or pass by many ways,
   By unnumbered ways of dream to death.

MYSTERY

WHY does this sudden passion smite me?
I stretch my hands, all blind to see:
I need the lamp of the world to light me,
    Lead me and set me free.

Something a moment seemed to stoop from
The night with cool, cool breath on my face:
Or did the hair of the twilight droop from
    Its silent wandering ways?

About me in the thick wood netted
The wizard glow looks human-wise;
And over the tree-tops barred and fretted
    Ponders with strange old eyes.

The tremulous lips of air blow by me
And hymn their time-old melody:
Its secret strain comes nigh and nigh me:
    "Ah, brother, come with me;

"For here the ancient mother lingers
To dip her hands in the diamond dew,
And lave thine ache with cloud-cool fingers
    Till sorrow die from you."

A NEW WORLD

I WHO had sought afar from earth
  The faery land to meet,
Now find content within its girth
  And wonder nigh my feet.

To-day a nearer love I choose
  And seek no distant sphere;
For aureoled by faery dews
  The dear brown breasts appear.

With rainbow radiance come and go
  The airy breaths of day;
And eve is all a pearly glow
  With moonlit winds a-play.

The lips of twilight burn my brow,
  The arms of night caress:
Glimmer her white eyes drooping now
  With grave old tenderness.

I close mine eyes from dream to be
  The diamond-rayed again,
As in the ancient hours ere we
  Forgot ourselves to men.

And all I thought of heaven before
  I find in earth below:
A sunlight in the hidden core
  To dim the noonday glow.

And with the earth my heart is glad,
  I move as one of old;
With mists of silver I am clad
  And bright with burning gold.

SACRIFICE

THOSE delicate wanderers,
The wind, the star, the cloud,
Ever before mine eyes,
As to an altar bowed,
Light and dew-laden airs
Offer in sacrifice.

The offerings arise:
Hazes of rainbow light,
Pure crystal, blue, and gold,
Through dreamland take their flight;
And 'mid the sacrifice
God moveth as of old.

In miracles of fire
He symbols forth his days;
In gleams of crystal light
Reveals what pure pathways
Lead to the soul's desire,
The silence of the height.

BROTHERHOOD

TWILIGHT, a blossom grey in shadowy valleys dwells:
Under the radiant dark the deep blue-tinted bells
In quietness reïmage heaven within their blooms,
Sapphire and gold and mystery. What strange perfumes,
Out of what deeps arising, all the flower-bells fling,
Unknowing the enchanted odorous song they sing!
Oh, never was an eve so living yet: the wood
Stirs not but breathes enraptured quietude.
Here in these shades the ancient knows itself, the soul,
And out of slumber waking starts unto the goal.
What bright companions nod and go along with it!
Out of the teeming dark what dusky creatures flit,
That through the long leagues of the island night above
Come by me, wandering, whispering, beseeching love;
As in the twilight children gather close and press
Nigh and more nigh with shadowy tenderness,
Feeling they know not what, with noiseless footsteps glide
Seeking familiar lips or hearts to dream beside.
O voices, I would go with you, with you, away,
Facing once more the radiant gateways of the day;
With you, with you, what memories arise, and nigh
Trampling the crowded figures of the dawn go by
Dread deities, the giant powers that warred on men
Grow tender brothers and gay children once again;
Fades every hate away before the Mother's breast
Where all the exiles of the heart return to rest.

ON A HILL-TOP

BEARDED with dewy grass the mountains thrust
Their blackness high into the still grey light,
Deepening to blue: far up the glimmering height
In silver transience shines the starry dust.

Silent the sheep about me; fleece by fleece
They sleep and stir not: I with awe around
Wander uncertain o'er the giant mound,
A fire that moves between their peace and peace.

The city myriads dream or sleep below;
Aloft another day has but begun:
Under the radiance of the Midnight Sun
The Tree of Life put forth its leaves to grow.

Wiser than they below who dream or sleep?
I know not; but their day is dream to me,
And in their darkness I awake to see
A Thought that moves like light within the deep.

Only from dream to dream our spirits pass:
Well, let us rise and fly from sphere to sphere;
Some one of all unto the light more near
Mirrors the Dreamer in its glowing glass.

THE VOICE OF THE WATERS

WHERE the Greyhound River windeth through a loneliness so deep,
Scarce a wild fowl shakes the quiet that the purple boglands keep,
Only God exults in silence over fields no man may reap.

Where the silver wave with sweetness fed the tiny lives of grass
I was bent above, my image mirrored in the fleeting glass,
And a voice from out the water through my being seemed to pass.

"Still above the waters brooding, spirit, in thy timeless quest;
Was the glory of thine image trembling over east and west
Not divine enough when mirrored in the morning water's breast?"

With the sighing voice that murmured I was borne to ages dim
Ere the void was lit with beauty breathed upon by seraphim,
We were cradled there together folded in the peace in Him.

One to be the master spirit, one to be the slave awoke,
One to shape itself obedient to the fiery words we spoke,
Flame and flood and stars and mountains from the primal waters broke.

I was huddled in the heather when the vision failed its light,
Still and blue and vast above me towered aloft the solemn height,
Where the stars like dewdrops glistened on the mountain slope of
night.

KRISHNA

(Imitated from a fragment of the Vaishnava Scriptures.)

I PAUSED beside the cabin door and saw the King of Kings at play,
Tumbled upon the grass I spied the little heavenly runaway.
The mother laughed upon the child made gay by its ecstatic morn,
And yet the sages spake of It as of the Ancient and Unborn.
I heard the passion breathed amid the honeysuckle scented glade,
And saw the King pass lightly from the beauty that he had betrayed.
I saw him pass from love to love; and yet the pure allowed His claim
To be the purest of the pure, thrice holy, stainless, without blame.
I saw the open tavern door flash on the dusk a ruddy glare,
And saw the King of Kings outcast reel brawling through the starlit air.
And yet He is the Prince of Peace of whom the ancient wisdom tells,
And by their silence men adore the lovely silence where He dwells.
I saw the King of Kings again, a thing to shudder at and fear,
A form so darkened and so marred that childhood fled if it drew near.
And yet He is the Light of Lights whose blossoming is Paradise,
That Beauty of the King which dawns upon the seers' enraptured eyes.
I saw the King of Kings again, a miser with a heart grown cold,
And yet He is the Prodigal, the Spendthrift of the Heavenly Gold,
The largesse of whose glory crowns the blazing brows of cherubim,
And sun and moon and stars and flowers are jewels scattered forth by Him.
I saw the King of Kings descend the narrow doorway to the dust
With all his fires of morning still, the beauty, bravery, and lust.
And yet He is the life within the Ever-living Living Ones,
The ancient with eternal youth, the cradle of the infant suns,
The fiery fountain of the stars, and He the golden urn where all
The glittering spray of planets in their myriad beauty fall.

FREEDOM

I WILL not follow you, my bird,
  I will not follow you.
I would not breathe a word, my bird,
  To bring thee here anew.

I love the free in thee, my bird,
  The lure of freedom drew;
The light you fly toward, my bird,
  I fly with thee unto.

And there we yet will meet, my bird,
  Though far I go from you
Where in the light outpoured, my bird,
  Are love and freedom too.

THE EARTH

THEY tell me that the earth is still the same
Although the Red Branch now is but a name,
That yonder peasant lifting up his eyes
Can see the marvel of the morning rise,
The wonder Deirdre gazed on when she came.

I cannot think the hearts that beat so high
Had not a lordlier palace roof of sky,
And that the earth on which the heroes trod
Seemed not to live beneath them like a god
Who loved them and could answer to their cry.

Who said the sun will shine with equal face
Alike upon the noble and the base?
The mighty only to the mighty seems;
The world that loomed through proud and golden dreams
Has dropped behind this world and left no trace.

When that the proud and golden race passed by,
This cold paternal majesty on high,
This unresponsive earth beneath the feet,
Replaced the dear brown breasts that were so sweet,
The face of brooding love within the sky.

How could a beggar wear the kingly crown,
Or those who weakly laid the sceptre down,
Walk 'mid the awful beauty God had made
For those whose hearts were proud and unafraid,
Careless if on His face were smile or frown?

TO ONE CONSECRATED

YOUR paths were all unknown to us:
We were so far away from you:
We mixed in thought your spirit thus—
With whiteness, stars of gold, and dew.

The Mighty Mother nourished you;
Her breath blew from her mystic bowers;
Their elfin glimmer floated through
The pureness of your shadowy hours.

The Mighty Mother made you wise,
Gave love that clears the hidden ways;
Her glooms were glory to your eyes,
Her darkness but the fount of days.

You with all gentleness she graced,
And beauty radiant as the morn's:
She made our joy in yours, then placed
Upon your head a crown of thorns.

Your eyes are filled with tender light
For those whose eyes are dim with tears:
They see your brow is crowned and bright,
But not its ring of wounding spears.

FORGIVENESS

AT dusk the window panes grew grey;
The wet world vanished in the gloom;
The dim and silver end of day
Scarce glimmered through the little room.

And all my sins were told; I said
Such things to her who knew not sin—
The sharp ache throbbing in my head,
The fever running high within.

I touched with pain her purity;
Sin's darker sense I could not bring:
My soul was black as night to me;
To her I was a wounded thing.

I needed love no words could say;
She drew me softly nigh her chair,
My head upon her knees to lay,
With cool hands that caressed my hair.

She sat with hands as if to bless,
And looked with grave, ethereal eyes;
Ensouled by ancient Quietness,
A gentle priestess of the Wise.

A WOMAN'S VOICE

HIS head within my bosom lay,
But yet his spirit slipped not through:
I only felt the burning clay
That withered for the cooling dew.

It was but pity when I spoke
And called him to my heart for rest,
And half a mother's love that woke
Feeling his head upon my breast:

And half the lion's tenderness
To shield her cubs from hurt or death,
Which, when the serried hunters press,
Makes terrible her wounded breath.

But when the lips I breathed upon
Asked for such love as equals claim—
I looked where all the stars were gone
Burned in the day's immortal flame.

"Come thou like yon great dawn to me
From darkness vanquished, battles done:
Flame unto flame shall flow and be
Within thy heart and mine as one.

THE SPIRIT OF THE GAY

WITH the glamour of the Gay
How you made our hearts to flame;
Gave each life some airy aim:
Ever round you seemed to play
Sunlight from some inner day.

Dazzling as with red and gold;
Rich with beauty, love and youth—
How were we to know the truth,
That if all the tale were told
Life for you was sad and cold?

For you found if we would wake
And the joy make young each heart,
You who told must stand apart:
And you bore it for our sake,
Though your heart was nigh to break.

So your life was like a sphere's:
One side, all aglow, meets day,
And the other turned away,
Icy-strange and cold appears,
Overhung with starry tears.

HEROIC LOVE

WHEN our glowing dreams were dead,
Ruined our heroic piles,
Something in your dark eyes said:
"Think no more of love or smiles."

Something in me still would say,
"Though our dreamland palace goes,
I have seen how in decay
Still the wild rose clings and blows."

But your dark eyes willed it thus:
"Build our lofty dream again:
Let our palace rise o'er us:
Love can never be till then."

DIVINE VISITATION

THE HEAVENS lay hold on us: the starry rays
Fondle with flickering fingers brow and eyes:
A new enchantment lights the ancient skies.
What is it looks between us gaze on gaze;
Does the wild spirit of the endless days
Chase through my heart some lure that ever flies?
Only I know the vast within me cries
Finding in thee the ending of all ways.
Ah, but they vanish; the immortal train
From thee, from me, depart, yet take from thee
Memorial grace: laden with adoration
Forth from this heart they flow that all in vain
Would stay the proud eternal powers that flee
After the chase in burning exultation.

PARTING

AS from our dream we died away
Far off I felt the outer things;
Your wind-blown tresses round me play,
Your bosom's gentle murmurings.

And far away our faces met
As on the verge of the vast spheres;
And in the night our cheeks were wet,
I could not say with dew or tears.

As one within the Mother's heart
In that hushed dream upon the height
We lived, and then we rose to part,
Because her ways are infinite.

NIGHT

BURNING our hearts out with longing
  The daylight passed:
Millions and millions together,
  The stars at last!

Purple the woods where the dewdrops,
  Pearly and grey,
Wash in the cool from our faces
  The flame of day.

Glory and shadow grow one in
  The hazel wood:
Laughter and peace in the stillness
  Together brood.

Hopes all unearthly are thronging
  In hearts of earth:
Tongues of the starlight are calling
  Our souls to birth.

Down from the heaven its secrets
  Drop one by one;
Where time is for ever beginning
  And time is done.

There light eternal is over
  Chaos and night:
Singing with dawn lips for ever,
  "Let there be light!"

There too for ever in twilight
  Time slips away,
Closing in darkness and rapture
  Its awful day.

DAWN SONG

WHILE the earth is dark and grey
How I laugh within. I know
In my breast what ardours gay
From the morning overflow.

Though the cheek be white and wet
In my heart no fear may fall:
There my chieftain leads and yet
Ancient battle trumpets call.

Bend on me no hasty frown
If my spirit slight your cares:
Sunlike still my joy looks down
Changing tears to beamy airs.

Think me not of fickle heart
If with joy my bosom swells
Though your ways from mine depart,
In the true are no farewells.

What I love in you I find
Everywhere. A friend I greet
In each flower and tree and wind—
Oh, but life is sweet, is sweet!

What to you are bolts and bars
Are to me the arms that guide
To the freedom of the stars,
Where my golden kinsmen bide.

From my mountain top I view:
Twilight's purple flower is gone,
And I send my song to you
On the level light of dawn.

THE HOUR OF THE KING

WHO would think this quiet breather
From the world had taken flight?
Yet within the form we see there
Wakes the Golden King to-night.

Out upon the face of faces
He looked forth before his sleep:
Now he knows the starry races
Haunters of the ancient deep.

On the Bird of Diamond Glory
Floats in mystic floods of song:
As he lists Time's triple story
Seems but as a day is long.

From the mightier Adam falling
To his image dwarfed in clay,
He will at our voices calling
Come to this side of the day.

When he wakes, the dreamy-hearted,
He will know not whence he came,
And the light from which he parted
Be the seraph's sword of flame,

And behind it hosts supernal
Guarding the lost paradise,
And the tree of life eternal
From the weeping human eyes.

THE HEROES

BY many a dream of God and man my thoughts in shining flocks were led:
But as I went through Patrick Street the hopes and prophecies were dead.
The hopes and prophecies were dead: they could not blossom where
   the feet
Walked amid rottenness, or where the brawling shouters stamped the
   street.
Where was the beauty that the Lord gave men when first they towered
   in pride?
But one came by me at whose word the bitter condemnation died.
His brows were crowned with thorns of light: his eyes were bright as
   one who sees
The starry palaces shine o'er the sparkle of the heavenly seas.
"Is it not beautiful?" he cried. "Our Faery Land of Hearts' Desire
Is mingled through the mire and mist, yet stainless keeps its lovely fire.
The pearly phantoms with blown hair are dancing where the drunkards
   reel:
The cloud frail daffodils shine out where filth is splashing from the heel.
O sweet, and sweet, and sweet to hear, the melodies in rivers run:
The rapture of their crowded notes is yet the myriad voice of One.
Those who are lost and fallen here, to-night in sleep shall pass the gate,
Put on the purples of the King, and know them masters of their fate.
Each wrinkled hag shall reassume the plumes and hues of paradise:
Each brawler be enthroned in calm among the Children of the Wise.
Yet in the council with the gods no one will falter to pursue
His lofty purpose, but come forth the cyclic labours to renew;
And take the burden of the world and veil his beauty in a shroud,
And wrestle with the chaos till the anarch to the light be bowed.
We cannot for forgetfulness forego the reverence due to them
Who wear at times they do not guess the sceptre and the diadem.
As bright a crown as this was theirs when first they from the Father sped;
Yet look with deeper eyes and still the ancient beauty is not dead."
He mingled with the multitude. I saw their brows were crowned and bright,
A light around the shadowy heads, a shadow round the head of light.

PAIN

MEN have made them gods of love,
Sun-gods, givers of the rain,
Deities of hill and grove:
I have made a god of Pain.

Of my god I know this much,
And in singing I repeat,
Though there's anguish in his touch,
Yet his soul within is sweet.

SELF-DISCIPLINE

WHEN the soul sought refuge in the place of rest,
Overborne by strife and pain beyond control,
From some secret hollow, whisper soft-confessed,
   Came the legend of the soul.

Some bright one of old time laid his sceptre down
So his heart might learn of sweet and bitter truth;
Going forth bereft of beauty, throne, and crown,
   And the sweetness of his youth.

So the old appeal and fierce revolt we make
Through the world's hour dies within our primal will;
And we justify the pain and hearts that break,
   And our lofty doom fulfil.

THE MAN TO THE ANGEL

I HAVE wept a million tears:
Pure and proud one, where are thine,
What the gain though all thy years
In unbroken beauty shine?

All your beauty cannot win
Truth we learn in pain and sighs:
You can never enter in
To the circle of the wise.

They are but the slaves of light
Who have never known the gloom,
And between the dark and bright
Willed in freedom their own doom.

Think not in your pureness there,
That our pain but follows sin:
There are fires for those who dare
Seek the throne of might to win.

Pure one, from your pride refrain:
Dark and lost amid the strife
I am myriad years of pain
Nearer to the fount of life.

When defiance fierce is thrown
At the god to whom you bow,
Rest the lips of the Unknown
Tenderest upon my brow.

A VISION OF BEAUTY

WHERE we sat at dawn together, while the star-rich heavens shifted,
We were weaving dreams in silence, suddenly the veil was lifted.
By a hand of fire awakened, in a moment caught and led
Upward to the heaven of heavens—through the star-mists overhead
Flare and flaunt the monstrous highlands; on the sapphire coast of night
Fall the ghostly froth and fringes of the ocean of the light.
Many coloured shine the vapours: to the moon-eye far away
'Tis the fairy ring of twilight, mid the spheres of night and day,
Girdling with a rainbow cincture round the planet where we go,
We and it together fleeting, poised upon the pearly glow;
We and it and all together flashing through the starry spaces
In a tempest dream of beauty lighting up the face of faces.
Half our eyes behold the glory; half within the spirit's glow
Echoes of the noiseless revels and the will of Beauty go.
By a hand of fire uplifted—to her star-strewn palace brought,
To the mystic heart of beauty and the secret of her thought:
Here of yore the ancient Mother in the fire mists sank to rest,
And she built her dreams about her, rayed from out her burning breast:
Here the wild will woke within her lighting up her flying dreams,
Round and round the planets whirling break in woods and flowers and
        streams,
And the winds are shaken from them as the leaves from off the rose,
And the feet of earth go dancing in the way that beauty goes,
And the souls of earth are kindled by the incense of her breath
As her light alternate lures them through the gates of birth and death.
O'er the fields of space together following her flying traces,
In a radiant tumult thronging, suns and stars and myriad races
Mount the spirit spires of beauty, reaching onward to the day
When the Shepherd of the Ages draws his misty hordes away
Through the glimmering deeps to silence, and within the awful fold
Life and joy and love forever vanish as a tale is told,
Lost within the Mother's being. So the vision flamed and fled,
And before the glory fallen every other dream lay dead.

THE VESTURE OF THE SOUL

I PITIED one whose tattered dress
Was patched, and stained with dust and rain;
He smiled on me; I could not guess
The viewless spirit's wide domain.

He said, "The royal robe I wear
Trails all along the fields of light:
Its silent blue and silver bear
For gems the starry dust of night.

"The breath of Joy unceasingly
Waves to and fro its folds starlit,
And far beyond earth's misery
I live and breathe the joy of it."

THE FREE

THEY bathed in the fire-flooded fountains:
Life girdled them round and about:
They slept in the clefts of the mountains:
The stars called them forth with a shout.

They prayed, but their worship was only
The wonder at nights and at days,
As still as the lips of the lonely
Though burning with dumbness of praise.

No sadness of earth ever captured
Their spirits who bowed at the shrine:
They fled to the Lonely enraptured
And hid in the darkness divine.

As children at twilight may gather,
They met at the doorway of death
The smile of the dark hidden Father,
The Mother with magical breath.

Untold of in song or in story,
In days long forgotten of men,
Their eyes were yet blind with a glory
Time will not remember again.

COMFORT

DARK head by the fireside brooding,
  Where upon your ears
Whirlwinds of the earth intruding
  Sound in wrath and tears:

Tender-hearted, in your lonely
  Sorrow I would fain
Comfort you, and say that only
  Gods could feel such pain.

Only spirits know such longing
  For the far away;
And the fiery fancies thronging
  Rise not out of clay.

Keep the secret sense celestial
  Of the starry birth;
Though about you call the bestial
  Voices of the earth.

If a thousand ages since
  Hurled us from the throne:
Then a thousand ages wins
  Back again our own.

Sad one, dry away your tears:
  Mount again anew:
In the great ancestral spheres
  Waits the throne for you.

WARNING

PURE at heart we wander now:
Comrade on the quest divine,
Turn not from the stars your brow
That your eyes may rest on mine.

Pure at heart we wander now:
We have hopes beyond to-day;
And our quest does not allow
Rest or dreams along the way.

We are, in our distant hope,
One with all the great and wise:
Comrade, do not turn or grope
For some lesser light that dies.

We must rise or we must fall:
Love can know no middle way:
If the great life do not call,
Then is sadness and decay.

DREAM LOVE

I DID not deem it half so sweet
To feel thy gentle hand,
As in a dream thy soul to greet
Across wide leagues of land.

Untouched more near to draw to you
Where, amid radiant skies,
Glimmered thy plumes of iris hue,
My Bird of Paradise.

Let me dream only with my heart,
Love first, and after see:
Know thy diviner counterpart
Before I kneel to thee.

So in thy motions all expressed
Thy angel I may view:
I shall not on thy beauty rest,
But beauty's self in you.

REFUGE

TWILIGHT a timid fawn, went glimmering by,
  And Night, the dark-blue hunter, followed fast,
Ceaseless pursuit and flight were in the sky,
  But the long chase had ceased for us at last.

We watched together while the driven fawn
  Hid in the golden thicket of the day.
We, from whose hearts pursuit and flight were gone,
  Knew on the hunter's breast her refuge lay.

THE BURNING-GLASS

A SHAFT of fire that falls like dew,
  And melts and maddens all my blood,
From out thy spirit flashes through
  The burning-glass of womanhood.

Only so far; here must I stay:
  Nearer I miss the light, the fire;
I must endure the torturing ray,
  And with all beauty, all desire.

Ah, time long must the effort be,
  And far the way that I must go
To bring my spirit unto thee,
  Behind the glass, within the glow.

BABYLON

THE BLUE dusk ran between the streets: my love was winged within
    my mind,
It left to-day and yesterday and thrice a thousand years behind.
To-day was past and dead for me, for from to-day my feet had run
Through thrice a thousand years to walk the ways of ancient Babylon.
On temple top and palace roof the burnished gold flung back the rays
Of a red sunset that was dead and lost beyond a million days.
The tower of heaven turns darker blue, a starry sparkle now begins;
The mystery and magnificence, the myriad beauty and the sins
Come back to me. I walk beneath the shadowy multitude of towers;
Within the gloom the fountain jets its pallid mist in lily flowers.
The waters lull me and the scent of many gardens, and I hear
Familiar voices, and the voice I love is whispering in my ear.
Oh real as in dream all this; and then a hand on mine is laid:
The wave of phantom time withdraws; and that young Babylonian maid,
One drop of beauty left behind from all the flowing of that tide,
Is looking with the self-same eyes, and here in Ireland by my side.
Oh light our life in Babylon, but Babylon has taken wings,
While we are in the calm and proud procession of eternal things.

THE FACES OF MEMORY

DREAM faces bloom around your face
  Like flowers upon one stem;
The heart of many a vanished race
  Sighs as I look on them.

The sun rich face of Egypt glows,
  The eyes of Eire brood,
With whom the golden Cyprian shows
  In lovely sisterhood.

Your tree of life put forth these flowers
  In ages past away:
They had the love in other hours
  I give to you to-day.

One light their eyes have, as may shine
  One star on many a sea,
They look that tender love on mine
  That lights your glance on me.

They fade in you; their lips are fain
  To meet the old caress:
And all their love is mine again
  As lip to lip we press.

THE MESSAGE

DO you not feel the white glow in your breast, my bird?
  That is the flame of love I send to you from afar:
Not a wafted kiss, hardly a whispered word,
  But love itself that flies as a white-winged star.

Let it dwell there, let it rest there, at home in your heart:
  Wafted on winds of gold, it is Love itself, the Dove.
Not the god whose arrows wounded with bitter smart,
  Nor the purple-fiery birds of death and love.

Do not ask for the hands of love or love's soft eyes:
  They give less than love who give all, giving what wanes.
I give you the star-fire, the heart-way to Paradise,
  With no death after, no arrow with stinging pains.

THE SINGING SILENCES

WHILE the yellow constellations shine with pale and tender glory,
In the lilac-scented stillness let us listen to earth's story.
All the flowers like moths a-flutter glimmer rich with dusky hues;
Everywhere around us seem to fall from nowhere the sweet dews.
Through the drowsy lull, the murmur, stir of leaf and sleepy hum,
We can feel a gay heart beating, hear a magic singing come.
Ah, I think that as we linger lighting at earth's olden fire
Fitful gleams in clay that perish, little sparks that soon expire:
So the Mother brims her gladness from a life beyond her own,
From whose darkness as a fountain up the fiery days are thrown;
Starry words that wheel in splendour, sunny systems, histories,
Vast and nebulous traditions told in the eternities.
And our listening Mother whispers through her children all the story.
Come: the yellow constellations shine with pale and tender glory!

AFFINITY

YOU and I have found the secret way,
None can bar our love or say us nay:
All the world may stare and never know
You and I are twined together so.

You and I for all his vaunted width
Know the giant Space is but a myth;
Over miles and miles of pure deceit
You and I have found our lips can meet.

You and I have laughed the leagues apart
In the soft delight of heart to heart.
If there's a gulf to meet or limit set,
You and I have never found it yet.

You and I have trod the backward way
To the happy heart of yesterday,
To the love we felt in ages past.
You and I have found it still to last.

You and I have found the joy had birth
In the angel childhood of the earth,
Hid within the heart of man and maid.
You and I of Time are not afraid.

You and I can mock his fabled wing,
For a kiss is an immortal thing.
And the throb wherein those old lips met
Is a living music in us yet.

A CALL

DUSK its ash-grey blossoms sheds on violet skies,
Over twilight mountains where the heart songs rise,
Rise and fall and fade away from earth to air.
Earth renews the music sweeter. Oh, come there.
Come, acushla, come, as in ancient times
Rings aloud the underland with faery chimes.
Down the unseen ways as strays each tinkling fleece
Winding ever onward to a fold of peace,
So my dreams go straying in a land more fair;
Half I tread the dew-wet grasses, half wander there.
Fade your glimmering eyes in a world grown cold;
Come, acushla, with me to the mountains old.
There the bright ones call us waving to and fro—
Come, my children, with me to the ancient go.

CARROWMORE

IT'S a lonely road through bogland to the lake at Carrowmore,
And a sleeper there lies dreaming where the water laps the shore;
Though the moth-wings of the twilight in their purples are unfurled,
Yet his sleep is filled with music by the masters of the world.

There's a hand is white as silver that is fondling with his hair:
There are glimmering feet of sunshine that are dancing by him there:
And half-open lips of faery that were dyed a faery red
In their revels where the Hazel Tree its holy clusters shed.

"Come away," the red lips whisper, "all the world is weary now;
'Tis the twilight of the ages and it's time to quit the plough.
Oh, the very sunlight's weary ere it lightens up the dew,
And its gold is changed and faded before it falls to you.

"Though your colleen's heart be tender, a tenderer heart is near.
What's the starlight in her glances when the stars are shining clear?
Who would kiss the fading shadow when the flower-face glows above?
'Tis the beauty of all Beauty that is calling for your love."

Oh, the great gates of the mountain have opened once again,
And the sound of song and dancing falls upon the ears of men,
And the Land of Youth lies gleaming, flushed with rainbow light and mirth,
And the old enchantment lingers in the honey-heart of earth.

THE DREAM OF THE CHILDREN

THE CHILDREN awoke in their dreaming
  While earth lay dewy and still:
They followed the rill in its gleaming
  To the heart-light of the hill.

Its sounds and sights were forsaking
  The world as they faded in sleep,
When they heard a music breaking
  Out from the heart-light deep.

It ran where the rill in its flowing
  Under the star-light gay,
With wonderful colour was glowing
  Like the bubbles they blew in their play.

From the misty mountain under
  Shot gleams of an opal star;
Its pathways of rainbow wonder
  Rayed to their feet from afar.

From their feet as they strayed in the meadow
  It led through caverned aisles,
Filled with purple and green light and shadow
  For mystic miles on miles.

The children were glad: it was lonely
  To play on the hillside by day.
"But now," they said, "we have only
  To go where the good people stray."

For all the hillside was haunted
  By the faery folk come again;
And down in the heart-light enchanted
  Were opal-coloured men.

They moved like kings unattended
  Without a squire or dame,
But they wore tiaras splendid
  With feathers of starlight flame.

They laughed at the children over
  And called them into the heart.
"Come down here, each sleepless rover;
  We will show you some of our art."

And down through the cool of the mountain
  The children sank at the call,
And stood in a blazing fountain
  And never a mountain at all.

The lights were coming and going
  In many a shining strand,
For the opal fire-kings were blowing
  The darkness out of the land.

This golden breath was a madness
  To set a poet on fire;
And this was a cure for sadness,
  And that the ease of desire.

They said as dawn glimmered hoary,
  "We will show yourselves for an hour."
And the children were changed to a glory
  By the beautiful magic of power.

The fire-kings smiled on their faces
  And called them by olden names,
Till they towered like the starry races
  All plumed with the twilight flames.

They talked for a while together
  How the toil of ages oppressed,
And of how they best could weather
  The ship of the world to its rest.

The dawn in the room was straying:
  The children began to blink,
When they heard a far voice saying
  "You can grow like that if you think."

The sun came in yellow and gay light:
  They tumbled out of the cot:
And half of the dream went with daylight
  And half was never forgot.

INSPIRATION

LIGHTEST of dancers, with no thought
Thy glimmering feet beat on my heart,
Gayest of singers, with no care
Waking to beauty the still air,
More than the labours of our art,
More than our wisdom can impart,
Thine idle ecstasy hath taught.

Lost long in solemn ponderings,
With the blind shepherd mind for guide,
The uncreated joy in you
Hath lifted up my heart unto
The morning stars in their first pride,
And the angelic joys that glide
High upon heaven-uplifted wings.

A MEMORY

YOU remember, dear, together
  Two children, you and I,
Sat once in the autumn weather,
  Watching the autumn sky.

There was some one round us straying
  The whole of the long day through,
Who seemed to say, "I am playing
  At hide and seek with you."

And one thing after another
  Was whispered out of the air,
How God was a big, kind brother
  Whose home is in everywhere.

His light like a smile comes glancing
  Through the cool, cool winds as they pass,
From the flowers in heaven dancing
  To the stars that shine in the grass.

From the clouds in deep blue wreathing
  And most from the mountains tall,
But God like a wind goes breathing
  A dream of Himself in all.

The heart of the Wise was beating
  Sweet, sweet, in our hearts that day:
And many a thought came fleeting
  And fancies solemn and gay.

We were grave in our way divining
  How childhood was taking wings,
And the wonder world was shining
  With vast eternal things.

The solemn twilight fluttered
  Like the plumes of seraphim,
And we felt what things were uttered
  In the sunset voice of Him.

We lingered long, for dearer
  Than home were the mountain places
Where God from the stars dropt nearer
  Our pale, dreamy faces.

Our very hearts from beating
  We stilled in awed delight,
For spirit and children were meeting
  In the purple, ample night.

A SUMMER NIGHT

HER mist of primroses within her breast
Twilight hath folded up, and o'er the west,
Seeking remoter valleys long hath gone,
Not yet hath come her sister of the dawn.
Silence and coolness now the earth enfold,
Jewels of glittering green, long mists of gold,
Hazes of nebulous silver veil the height,
And shake in tremors through the shadowy night.
Heard through the stillness, as in whispered words,
The wandering God-guided wings of birds
Ruffle the dark. The little lives that lie
Deep hid in grass join in a long-drawn sigh
More softly still; and unheard through the blue
The falling of innumerable dew,
Lifts with grey fingers all the leaves that lay
Burned in the heat of the consuming day.
The lawns and lakes lie in this night of love,
Admitted to the majesty above.
Earth with the starry company hath part;
The waters hold all heaven within their heart,
And glimmer o'er with wave-lips everywhere
Lifted to meet the angel lips of air.
The many homes of men shine near and far,
Peace-laden as the tender evening star,
The late home-coming folk anticipate
Their rest beyond the passing of the gate,
And tread with sleep-filled hearts and drowsy feet.
Oh, far away and wonderful and sweet
All this, all this. But far too many things
Obscuring, as a cloud of seraph wings
Blinding the seeker for the Lord behind,
I fall away in weariness of mind.
And think how far apart are I and you,
Beloved, from those spirit children who
Felt but one single Being long ago,
Whispering in gentleness and leaning low
Out of its majesty, as child to child.
I think upon it all with heart grown wild.
Hearing no voice, howe'er my spirit broods,
No whisper from the dense infinitudes,

This world of myriad things whose distance awes.
Ah me; how innocent our childhood was!

THE WEAVER OF SOULS

WHO is this unseen messenger
For ever between me and her,
Who brings love's precious merchandise,
The golden breath, the dew of sighs,
And the wild, gentle thoughts that dwell
Too fragile for the lips to tell,
Each at their birth, to us before
A heaving of the heart is o'er?
Who art thou, unseen messenger?

I think, O Angel of the Lord,
You make our hearts to so accord
That those who hear in after hours
May sigh for love as deep as ours;
And seek the magic that can give
An Eden where the soul may live,
Nor need to walk a road of clay
With stumbling feet, nor fall away
From thee, O Angel of the Lord.

THE SILENCE OF LOVE

I COULD praise you once with beautiful words ere you came
And entered my life with love in a wind of flame.
I could lure with a song from afar my bird to its nest,
But with pinions drooping together silence is best.

In the land of beautiful silence the winds are laid,
And life grows quietly one in the cloudy shade.
I will not waken the passion that sleeps in the heart,
For the winds that blew us together may blow us apart.

Fear not the stillness; for doubt and despair shall cease
With the gentle voices guiding us into peace.
Our dreams will change as they pass through the gates of gold,
And Quiet, the tender shepherd, shall keep the fold.

CREATION

AS one by one the veils took flight,
The day withdrew, the stars came up.
The spirit issued pale and bright
Filling thy beauty like a cup.

Sacred thy laughter on the air,
Holy thy lightest word that fell,
Proud the innumerable hair
That waved at the enchanter's spell.

O, Master of the Beautiful,
Creating us from hour to hour,
Give me this vision to the full
To see in lightest things thy power.

This vision give, no heaven afar,
No throne, and yet I will rejoice
Knowing beneath my feet a star
Thy word in every wandering voice.

THE WINDS OF ANGUS

THE GREY road whereupon we trod became as holy ground:
The eve was all one voice that breathed its message with no sound:
And burning multitudes pour through my heart, too bright, too blind,
Too swift and hurried in their flight to leave their tale behind.
Twin gates unto that living world, dark honey-coloured eyes,
The lifting of whose lashes flushed the face with Paradise,
Beloved, there I saw within their ardent rays unfold
The likeness of enraptured birds that flew from deeps of gold
To deeps of gold within my breast to rest, or there to be
Transfigured in the light, or find a death to life in me.
So love, a burning multitude, a seraph wind that blows
From out the deep of being to the deep of being goes.
And sun and moon and starry fires and earth and air and sea
Are creatures from the deep let loose, who pause in ecstasy,
Or wing their wild and heavenly way until again they find
The ancient deep, and fade therein, enraptured, bright, and blind.

. APHRODITE

NOT unremembering we pass our exile from the starry ways:
One timeless hour in time we caught from the long night of endless days.
With solemn gaiety the stars danced far withdrawn on elfin heights:
The lilac breathed amid the shade of green and blue and citron lights.
But yet the close enfolding night seemed on the phantom verge of things,
For our adoring hearts had turned within from all their wanderings:
For beauty called to beauty, and there thronged at the enchanter's will
The vanished hours of love that burn within the Ever-living still.
And sweet eternal faces put the shadows of the earth to rout,
And faint and fragile as a moth your white hand fluttered and went out.
Oh, who am I who tower beside this goddess of the twilight air?
The burning doves fly from my heart, and melt within her bosom there.
I know the sacrifice of old they offered to the mighty queen,
And this adoring love has brought us back the beauty that has been.
As to her worshippers she came descending from her glowing skies,
So Aphrodite I have seen with shining eyes look through your eyes:
One gleam of the ancestral face which lighted up the dawn for me:
One fiery visitation of the love the gods desire in thee!

THE MEMORY OF EARTH

IN the wet dusk silver sweet,
Down the violet scented ways,
As I moved with quiet feet
I was met by mighty days.

On the hedge the hanging dew
Glassed the eve and stars and skies;
While I gazed a madness grew
Into thundered battle cries.

Where the hawthorn glimmered white,
Flashed the spear and fell the stroke—
Ah, what faces pale and bright
Where the dazzling battle broke!

There a hero-hearted queen
With young beauty lit the van:
Gone! the darkness flowed between
All the ancient wars of man.

While I paced the valley's gloom
Where the rabbits pattered near,
Shone a temple and a tomb
With the legend carven clear:

"Time put by a myriad fates
That her day might dawn in glory;
Death made wide a million gates
So to close her tragic story."

THE VEILS OF MAYA

MOTHER, with whom our lives should be,
Not hatred keeps our lives apart:
Charmed by some lesser glow in thee,
Our hearts beat not within thy heart.

Beauty, the face, the touch, the eyes,
Prophets of thee, allure our sight
From that unfathomed deep where lies
Thine ancient loveliness and light.

Self-found at last, the joy that springs
Being thyself, shall once again
Start thee upon the whirling rings
And through the pilgrimage of pain.

IN THE WOMB

STILL rests the heavy share on the dark soil:
Upon the black mould thick the dew-damp lies:
The horse waits patient: from his lowly toil
The ploughboy to the morning lifts his eyes.

The unbudding hedgerows dark against day's fires
Glitter with gold-lit crystals: on the rim
Over the unregarding city's spires
The lonely beauty shines alone for him.

And day by day the dawn or dark enfolds
And feeds with beauty eyes that cannot see
How in her womb the mighty mother moulds
The infant spirit for eternity.

SUNG ON A BY-WAY

WHAT of all the will to do?
  It has vanished long ago,
For a dream-shaft pierced it through
  From the Unknown Archer's bow.

What of all the soul to think?
  Some one offered it a cup
Filled with a diviner drink,
  And the flame has burned it up.

What of all the hope to climb?
  Only in the self we grope
To the misty end of time:
  Truth has put an end to hope.

What of all the heart to love?
  Sadder than for will or soul,
No light lured it on above;
  Love has found itself the whole.

JANUS

IMAGE of beauty, when I gaze on thee,
Trembling I waken to a mystery,
How through one door we go to life or death
By spirit kindled or the sensual breath.

Image of beauty, when my way I go;
No single joy or sorrow do I know:
Elate for freedom leaps the starry power,
The life which passes mourns its wasted hour.

And, ah, to think how thin the veil that lies
Between the pain of hell and paradise!
Where the cool grass my aching head embowers
God sings the lovely carol of the flowers.

THE GREY EROS

WE are desert leagues apart;
  Time is misty ages now
Since the warmth of heart to heart
  Chased the shadows from my brow.

Oh, I am so old, meseems
  I am next of kin to Time,
The historian of her dreams
  From the long-forgotten prime.

You have come a path of flowers.
  What a way was mine to roam!
Many a fallen empire's towers,
  Many a ruined heart my home.

No, there is no comfort, none.
  All the dewy tender breath
Idly falls when life is done
  On the starless brow of death.

Though the dream of love may tire,
  In the ages long agone
There were ruby hearts of fire—
  Ah, the daughters of the dawn!

Though I am so feeble now,
  I remember when our pride
Could not to the Mighty bow;
  We would sweep His stars aside.

Mix thy youth with thoughts like those—
  It were but to wither thee,
But to graft the youthful rose
  On the old and flowerless tree.

Age is no more near than youth
  To the sceptre and the crown.
Vain the wisdom, vain the truth;
  Do not lay thy rapture down.

DUALITY

From me spring good and evil.

WHO gave thee such a ruby flaming heart
And such a pure cold spirit? Side by side
I know these must eternally abide
In intimate war, and each to each impart
Life from its pain, in every joy a dart
To wound with grief or death the self allied.
Red life within the spirit crucified,
The eyes eternal pity thee: thou art
Fated with deathless powers at war to be,
Not less the martyr of the world than he
Whose thorn-crowned brow usurps the due of tears
We would pay to thee, ever ruddy life,
Whose passionate peace is still to be at strife,
O'erthrown but in the unconflicting spheres.

TRUTH

THE HERO first thought it
To him 'twas a deed:
To those who retaught it,
A chain on their speed.

The fire that we kindled,
A beacon by night,
When darkness has dwindled
Grows pale in the light.

For life has no glory
Stays long in one dwelling,
And time has no story
That's true twice in telling.

And only the teaching
That never was spoken
Is worthy thy reaching,
The fountain unbroken.

FANTASY

OVER all the dream-built margin, flushed with grey and hoary light,
Glint the bubble planets tossing in the dead black sea of night.
Immemorial face, how many faces look from out thy skies,
Now with ghostly eyes of wonder rimmed around with rainbow dyes:
Now the secrets of the future trail along the silent spheres:
Ah, how often have I followed filled with phantom hopes and fears,
Where my star that rose dream-laden, moving to the mystic crown,
On the yellow moon-rock foundered and my joy and dreams went down.
As a child with hands uplifted peering through the cloudless miles
Bent the Mighty Mother o'er me shining all with eyes and smiles:
"Come up hither, child, my darling": waving to the habitations,
Thrones, and starry kings around her, dark embattled planet nations.
There the mighty rose in greeting, as their child from exile turning
Smiled upon the awful faces o'er the throne supernal burning.
As with sudden sweetness melting, shone the eyes, the hearts of home,
Changed the vision, and the Mother vanished in the vasty dome.
So from marvel unto marvel turned the face I gazed upon,
Till its fading majesty grew tender as a child at dawn,
And the heaven of heavens departed and the visions passed away
With the seraph of the darkness martyred in the fires of day.

THE MOUNTAINEER

OH, at the eagle's height
To lie i' the sweet of the sun,
While veil after veil takes flight
And God and the world are one.

Oh, the night on the steep!
All that his eyes saw dim
Grows light in the dusky deep,
And God is alone with him.

THE GOLDEN AGE

WHEN the morning breaks above us
And the wild sweet stars have fled,
By the faery hands that love us
Wakened you and I will tread

Where the lilacs on the lawn
Shine with all their silver dews,
In the stillness of a dawn
Wrapped in tender primrose hues.

We will hear the strange old song
That the earth croons in her breast,
Echoed by the feathered throng
Joyous from each leafy nest.

Earth, whose dreams are we and they,
With her heart's deep gladness fills
All our human lips can say,
Or the dawn-fired singer trills.

She is rapt in dreams divine:
As her clouds of beauty pass,
On our glowing hearts they shine,
Mirrored there as in a glass.

So when all the vapours grey
From our flowery paths shall flit,
And the dawn begin the day,
We will sing that song to it

Ere its yellow fervour flies.—
Oh, we are so glad of youth,
Whose first sweetness never dies
Nourished by eternal truth.

THE MASTER SINGER

A LAUGHTER in the diamond air, a music in the trembling grass;
And one by one the words of light as joydrops through my being pass:
"I am the sunlight in the heart, the silver moon-glow in the mind;
My laughter runs and ripples through the wavy tresses of the wind.
I am the fire upon the hills, the dancing flame that leads afar
Each burning-hearted wanderer, and I the dear and homeward star.
A myriad lovers died for me, and in their latest yielded breath
I woke in glory giving them immortal life though touched by death.
They knew me from the dawn of time: if Hermes beats his rainbow wings,
If Angus shakes his locks of light, or golden-haired Apollo sings,
It matters not the name, the land: my joy in all the gods abides:
Even in the cricket in the grass some dimness of me smiles and hides.
For joy of me the daystar glows, and in delight and wild desire
The peacock twilight rays aloft its plumes and blooms of shadowy fire,
Where in the vastness too I burn through summer nights and ages long,
And with the fiery-footed watchers shake in myriad dance and song."

INHERITANCE

AS flow the rivers to the sea
Adown from rocky hill or plain,
A thousand ages toiled for thee
And gave thee harvest of their gain;
And weary myriads of yore
Dug out for thee earth's buried ore.

The shadowy toilers for thee fought
In chaos of primeval day
Blind battles with they knew not what;
And each before he passed away
Gave clear articulate cries of woe:
Your pain is theirs of long ago.

And all the old heart sweetness sung,
The joyous life of man and maid
In forests when the earth was young,
In rumours round your childhood strayed:
The careless sweetness of your mind
Comes from the buried years behind.

And not alone unto your birth
Their gifts the weeping ages bore,
The old descents of God on earth
Have dowered thee with celestial lore:
So, wise, and filled with sad and gay
You pass unto the further day.

IN AS MUCH ...

WHEN for love it was fain of
The wild heart was chidden,
When the white limbs were clothed
And the beauty was hidden;

For the scorn that was done to
The least of her graces,
The Mother veiled over
And hid from our faces

The high soul of nature,
The deep and the wonder,
Her towers up in heaven,
And the fairyland under.

The Mother then whispered,
"The wrong done by thee
To the least limb of beauty
Was done unto me."

THE SEER

OH, if my spirit may foretell
  Or earlier impart,
It is because I always dwell
  With morning in my heart.

I feel the keen embrace of light
  Ere dawning on the view
It sprays the chilly fold of night
  With iridescent dew.

The robe of dust around it cast
  Hides not the earth below,
Its heart of ruby flame, the vast
  Mysterious gloom and glow.

Something beneath yon coward gaze
  Betrays the royal line;
Its lust and hate, but errant rays,
  Are at their root divine.

I hail the light of elder years
  Behind the niggard mould,
The fiery kings, the seraph seers,
  As in the age of gold.

And all about and through the gloom
  Breaths from the golden clime
Are wafted like a sweet perfume
  From some most ancient time.

A NEW BEING

I KNOW myself no more, my child,
  Since thou art come to me,
Pity so tender and so wild
  Hath wrapped my thoughts of thee.

These thoughts, a fiery gentle rain,
  Are from the Mother shed,
Where many a broken heart hath lain
  And many a weeping head.

LIGHT AND DARK

NOT the soul that's whitest
  Wakens love the sweetest:
When the heart is lightest
  Oft the charm is fleetest.

While the snow-frail maiden,
  Waits the time of learning,
To the passion laden
  Turn with eager yearning.

While the heart is burning
  Heaven with earth is banded:
To the stars returning
  Go not empty-handed.

Ah, the snow-frail maiden!
  Somehow truth has missed her,
Left the heart unladen
  For its burdened sister.

RECALL

WHAT call may draw thee back again,
  Lost dove, what art, what charm may please?
The tender touch, the kiss, are vain,
  For thou wert lured away by these.

Oh, must we use the iron hand,
  And mask with hate the holy breath,
With alien voice give love's command,
  As they through love the call of death?

A LEADER

THOUGH your eyes with tears were blind,
Pain upon the path you trod:
Well we knew, the hosts behind,
Voice and shining of a god.

For your darkness was our day:
Signal fires, your pains untold
Lit us on our wandering way
To the mystic heart of gold.

Naught we knew of the high land,
Beauty burning in its spheres;
Sorrow we could understand
And the mystery told in tears.

THE LAST HERO

WE laid him to rest with tenderness;
Homeward we turned in the twilight's gold;
We thought in ourselves with dumb distress—
All the story of earth is told.

A beautiful word at the last was said:
A great deep heart like the hearts of old
Went forth; and the speaker had lost the thread,
Or all the story of earth was told.

The dust hung over the pale dry ways
Dizzily fired with the twilight's gold,
And a bitter remembrance blew in each face
How all the story of earth was told.

THE PAIN OF EARTH

DOES the earth grow grey with grief
For her hero darling fled?
Though her vales let fall no leaf,
In our hearts her tears are shed.

Still the stars laugh on above:
Not to them her grief is said;
Mourning for her hero love
In our hearts the tears are shed.

We her children mourn for him,
Mourn the elder hero dead;
In the twilight grey and dim
In our hearts the tears are shed.

UNCONSCIOUS

THE WINDS, the stars, and the skies though wrought
By the heavenly King yet know it not;
And man who moves in the twilight dim
Feels not the love that encircles him,
Though in heart, on bosom, and eyelids press
Lips of an infinite tenderness,
He turns away through the dark to roam
Nor heeds the fire in his hearth and home.

LOVE

ERE I lose myself in the vastness and drowse myself with the peace,
While I gaze on the light and the beauty afar from the dim homes of men,
May I still feel the heart-pang and pity, love-ties that I would not release;
May the voices of sorrow appealing call me back to their succour again.

Ere I storm with the tempest of power the thrones and dominions of old,
Ere the ancient enchantment allure me to roam through the star-misty skies,
I would go forth as one who has reaped well what harvest the earth
    may unfold;
May my heart be o'erbrimmed with compassion; on my brow be the
    crown of the wise.

I would go as the dove from the ark sent forth with wishes and prayers
To return with the paradise blossoms that bloom in the Eden of light:
When the deep star-chant of the seraphs I hear in the mystical airs,
May I capture one tone of their joy for the sad ones discrowned in the
    night.

Not alone, not alone would I go to my rest in the heart of the love:
Were I tranced in the innermost beauty, the flame of its tenderest breath,
I would still hear the cry of the fallen recalling me back from above,
To go down to the side of the people who weep in the shadow of death.

OM

A Memory

FAINT grew the yellow buds of light
Far flickering beyond the snows,
As leaning o'er the shadowy white
Morn glimmered like a pale primrose.

Within an Indian vale below
A child said "OM" with tender heart,
Watching with loving eyes the glow
In dayshine fade and night depart.

The word which Brahma at his dawn
Outbreathes and endeth at his night,
Whose tide of sound so rolling on
Gives birth to orbs of pearly light;

And beauty, wisdom, love, and youth,
By its enchantment gathered grow
In agelong wandering to the truth,
Through many a cycle's ebb and flow.

And here the voice of earth was stilled,
The child was lifted to the Wise:
A strange delight his spirit filled,
And Brahm looked from his shining eyes.

INDIAN SONG

SHADOWY-PETALLED, like the lotus, loom the mountains with
    their snows:
Through the sapphire Soma rising such a flood of glory throws
As when first in yellow splendour Brahma from the Lotus rose.

High above the darkening mounds where fade the fairy lights of day,
All the tiny planet folk are waving us from far away;
Thrilled by Brahma's breath they sparkle with the magic of the gay.

Brahma, all alone in gladness, dreams the joys that throng in space,
Shepherds all the whirling splendours onward to their resting place,
Where in worlds of lovely silence fade in one the starry race.

THE NUTS OF KNOWLEDGE

A CABIN on the mountain side hid in a grassy nook
Where door and windows open wide that friendly stars may look.
The rabbit shy can patter in, the winds may enter free,
Who throng around the mountain throne in living ecstasy.

And when the sun sets dimmed in eve and purple fills the air,
I think the sacred Hazel Tree is dropping berries there
From starry fruitage waved aloft where Connla's Well o'erflows;
For sure the enchanted waters run through every wind that blows.

I think when night towers up aloft and shakes the trembling dew,
How every high and lonely thought that thrills my being through
Is but a ruddy berry dropped down through the purple air,
And from the magic tree of life the fruit falls everywhere.

CHILDREN OF LIR

WE woke from our sleep in the bosom where cradled together we lay:
The love of the dark hidden Father went with us upon our way.
And gay was the breath in our being, and never a sorrow or fear
Was on us as, singing together, we flew from the infinite Lir.

Through nights lit with diamond and sapphire we raced with the
      children of dawn,
A chain that was silver and golden linked spirit to spirit, my swan,
Till day in the heavens passed over, and still grew the beat of our wings,
And the breath of the darkness enfolded to teach us unspeakable things.

Yet lower we fell and for comfort our pinionless spirits had now
The leaning of bosom to bosom, the lifting of lip unto brow.
Though chained to the earth yet we mourned not the loss of our
      heaven above,
But passed from the vision of beauty to the fathomless being of love.

Still gay is the breath in our being, we wait for the bell branch to ring
To call us away to the Father, and then we will rise on the wing,
And fly through the twilights of time till the home lights of heaven appear;
Our spirits through love and through longing made one in the infinite Lir.

PRAYER

LET us leave our island woods grown dim and blue;
O'er the waters creeping the pearl dust of the eve
Hides the silver of the long wave rippling through:
    The chill for the warm room let us leave.

Turn the lamp down low and draw the curtain wide,
So the greyness of the starlight bathes the room;
Let us see the giant face of night outside,
    Though vague as a moth's wing is the gloom.

Rumour of the fierce-pulsed city far away
Breaks upon the peace that aureoles our rest,
Steeped in stillness as if some primeval day
    Hung drowsily o'er the water's breast.

Shut the eyes that flame and hush the heart that burns:
In quiet we may hear the old primeval cry:
God gives wisdom to the spirit that upturns:
    Let us adore now, you and I.

Age on age is heaped about us as we hear:
Cycles hurry to and fro with giant tread
From the deep unto the deep: but do not fear,
    For the soul unhearing them is dead.

BENEDICTION

NOW the rooftree of the midnight spreading,
  Buds in citron, green, and blue:
From afar its mystic odours shedding,
    Child, on you.

Now the buried stars beneath the mountain
  And the vales their life renew,
Jetting rainbow blooms from tiny fountains,
    Child, for you.

In the diamond air the sun-star glowing,
  Up its feathered radiance threw;
All the jewel glory there was flowing,
    Child, for you.

As within the quiet waters passing,
  Sun and moon and stars we view,
So the loveliness of life is glassing,
    Child, in you.

And the fire divine in all things burning
  Seeks the mystic heart anew,
From its wanderings far again returning,
    Child, to you.

THE MID-WORLD

THIS is the red, red region
Your heart must journey through:
Your pains will here be legion
And joy be death for you.

Rejoice to-day: to-morrow
A turning tide shall flow
Through infinite tones of sorrow
To reach an equal woe.

You pass by love unheeding
To gain the goal you long—
But my heart, my heart is bleeding:
I cannot sing this song.

REMEMBRANCE

THERE were many burning hours on the heartsweet tide,
  And we passed away from ourselves, forgetting all
The immortal moods that faded, the god who died,
  Hastening away to the King on a distant call.

There were ruby dews were shed when the heart was riven,
  And passionate pleading and prayers to the dead we had wronged;
And we passed away, unremembering and unforgiven,
  Hastening away to the King for the peace we longed.

Love unremembered and heart-ache we left behind,
  We forsook them, unheeding, hastening away in our flight;
We knew the hearts we had wronged of old we would find
  When we came to the fold of the King for rest in the night.

THE VISION OF LOVE

THE TWILIGHT fleeted away in pearl on the stream,
And night, like a diamond done, stood still in our dream.
Your eyes like burnished stones or as stars were bright
With the sudden vision that made us one with the night.

We loved in infinite spaces, forgetting here
The breasts that were lit with life and the lips so near;
Till the wizard willows waved in the wind and drew
Me away from the fulness of love and down to you.

Our love was so vast that it filled the heavens up:
But the soft white form I held was an empty cup,
When the willows called me back to earth with their sigh,
And we moved as shades through the deep that was you and I.

THE CHRIST-SWORD

THE WHILE my mad brain whirled around
She only looked with eyes elate
Immortal love at me. I found
How deep the glance of love can wound,
How cruel pity is to hate.

I was begirt with hostile spears:
My angel warred in me for you
Whose gentle calmness all too fierce
Made unseen lightnings to pierce
My heart that dripped with ruddy dew.

I know how on the final day
The hosts of darkness meet with death:
The angels with their love shall slay,
Flowing to meet the dark array
With terrible yet tender breath.

BLINDNESS

OUR true hearts are forever lonely:
A wistfulness is in our thought:
Our lights are like the dawns which only
Seem bright to us and yet are not.

Something you see in me I wis not:
Another heart in you I guess:
A stranger's lips—but thine I kiss not,
Erring in all my tenderness.

I sometimes think a mighty lover
Takes every burning kiss we give:
His lights are those which round us hover:
For him alone our lives we live.

Ah, sigh for us whose hearts unseeing
Point all their passionate love in vain,
And blinded in the joy of being,
Meet only when pain touches pain.

WHOM WE WORSHIP

I WOULD not have the love of lips and eyes,
    The ancient ways of love:
But in my heart I built a Paradise,
    A nest there for the dove.

I felt the wings of light that fluttered through
    The gate I held apart:
And all without was shadow, but I knew
    The bird within my heart.

Then, while the innermost with music beat,
    The voice I loved so long
Seemed only the dream echo faint and sweet
    Of a far sweeter song.

I could not even bear the thought I felt
    Of Thee and Me therein;
And with white heat I strove the veil to melt
    That love to love might win.

But ah, my dreams within their fountain fell;
    Not to be lost in thee,
But with the high ancestral love to dwell
    In its lone ecstasy.

REFLECTIONS

HOW shallow is this mere that gleams!
Its depth of blue is from the skies,
And from a distant sun the dreams
And lovely light within your eyes.

We deem our love so infinite
Because the Lord is everywhere,
And love awakening is made bright
And bathed in that diviner air.

We go on our enchanted way
And deem our hours immortal hours,
Who are but shadow kings that play
With mirrored majesties and powers.

THE MORNING STAR

IN the black pool of the midnight Lu has slung the morning star,
And its foam in rippling silver whitens into day afar
Falling on the mountain rampart piled with pearl above our glen,
Only you and I, beloved, moving in the fields of men.

In the dark tarn of my spirit, love, the morning star, is lit;
And its halo, ever brightening, lightens into dawn in it.
Love, a pearl-grey dawn in darkness, breathing peace without desire;
But I fain would shun the burning terrors of the mid-day fire.

Through the faint and tender airs of twilight star on star may gaze,
But the eyes of light are blinded in the white flame of the days,
From the heat that melts together oft a rarer essence slips,
And our hearts may still be parted in the meeting of the lips.

What a darkness would I gaze on when the day had passed the west,
If my eyes were dazed and blinded by the whiteness of a breast?
Never through the diamond darkness could I hope to see afar
Where beyond the pearly rampart burned the purer evening star.

ILLUSION

WHAT is the love of shadowy lips
That know not what they seek or press,
From whom the lure for ever slips
And fails their phantom tenderness?

The mystery and light of eyes
That near to mine grow dim and cold;
They move afar in ancient skies
Mid flame and mystic darkness rolled.

O beauty, as thy heart o'erflows
In tender yielding unto me,
A vast desire awakes and grows
Unto forgetfulness of thee.

THE DREAM

I WOKE to find my pillow wet
  With the tears for deeds deep hid in sleep.
I knew no sorrow here, but yet
  The tears fell softly through the deep.

Your eyes, your other eyes of dream,
  Looked at me through the veil of blank;
I saw their joyous, starlit gleam
  Like one who watches rank on rank.

His victor airy legions wind
  And pass before his awful throne—
Was there thy loving heart unkind,
  Was I thy captive all o'erthrown?

MISTRUST

YOU look at me with wan, bright eyes
  When in the deeper world I stray:
You fear some hidden ambush lies
  In wait to call me, "Come away."

What if I see behind the veil
  Your starry self beseeching me,
Or at its stern command grow pale,
  "Let her be free, let her be free"?

ALIEN

DARK glowed the vales of amethyst
Beneath an opal shroud:
The moon bud opened through the mist
Its white-fire leaves of cloud.

Through rapt at gaze with eyes of light
Looked forth the seraph seers,
The vast and wandering dream of night
Rolled on above our tears.

THE TIDE OF SORROW

ON the twilight-burnished hills I lie and long and gaze
Where below the grey-lipped sands drink in the flowing tides,
Drink, and fade and disappear: interpreting their ways
   A seer in my heart abides.

Once the diamond dancing day-waves laved thy thirsty lips:
Now they drink the dusky night-tide running cold and fleet,
Drink, and as the chilly brilliance o'er their pallor slips
   They fade in the touch they meet.

Wave on wave of pain where leaped of old the billowy joys:
Hush and still thee now unmoved to drink the bitter sea,
Drink with equal heart: be brave; and life with laughing voice
   And death will be one for thee.

Ere my mortal days pass by and life in the world be done,
Oh, to know what world shall rise within the spirit's ken
When it grows into the peace where light and dark are one!
   What voice for the world of men?

WEARINESS

WHERE are now the dreams divine,
Fires that lit the dawning soul,
As the ruddy colours shine
Through an opal aureole?

Moving in a joyous trance,
We were like the forest glooms
Rumorous of old romance,
Fraught with unimagined dooms.

Titans we or morning stars,
So we seemed in days of old,
Mingling in the giant wars
Fought afar in deeps of gold.

God, an elder brother dear,
Filled with kindly light our thought:
Many a radiant form was near
Whom our hearts remember not.

Would they know us now? I think
Old companions of the prime
From our garments well might shrink,
Muddied with the lees of Time.

Fade the heaven-assailing moods:
Slave to petty tasks I pine
For the quiet of the woods,
And the sunlight seems divine.

And I yearn to lay my head
Where the grass is green and sweet,
Mother, all the dreams are fled
From the tired child at thy feet.

THE TWILIGHT OF EARTH

THE WONDER of the world is o'er:
  The magic from the sea is gone:
There is no unimagined shore,
  No islet yet to venture on.
The Sacred Hazels' blooms are shed,
The Nuts of Knowledge harvested.

Oh, what is worth this lore of age
  If time shall never bring us back
Our battle with the gods to wage
  Reeling along the starry track.
The battle rapture here goes by
In warring upon things that die.

Let be the tale of him whose love
  Was sighed between white Deirdre's breasts,
It will not lift the heart above
  The sodden clay on which it rests.
Love once had power the gods to bring
All rapt on its wild wandering.

We shiver in the falling dew,
  And seek a shelter from the storm:
When man these elder brothers knew
  He found the mother nature warm,
A hearth fire blazing through it all,
A home without a circling wall.

We dwindle down beneath the skies,
  And from ourselves we pass away:
The paradise of memories
  Grows ever fainter day by day.
The shepherd stars have shrunk within,
The world's great night will soon begin.

Will no one, ere it is too late,
  Ere fades the last memorial gleam,
Recall for us our earlier state?
  For nothing but so vast a dream
That it would scale the steeps of air
Could rouse us from so vast despair.

The power is ours to make or mar
  Our fate as on the earliest morn,
The Darkness and the Radiance are
  Creatures within the spirit born.
Yet, bathed in gloom too long, we might
Forget how we imagined light.

Not yet are fixed the prison bars;
  The hidden light the spirit owns
If blown to flame would dim the stars
  And they who rule them from their thrones:
And the proud sceptred spirits thence
Would bow to pay us reverence.

Oh, while the glory sinks within
  Let us not wait on earth behind,
But follow where it flies, and win
  The glow again, and we may find
Beyond the Gateways of the Day
Dominion and ancestral sway.

THE GARDEN OF GOD

WITHIN the iron cities
One walked unknown for years,
In his heart the pity of pities
That grew for human tears.

When love and grief were ended
The flower of pity grew:
By unseen hands 't was tended
And fed with holy dew.

Though in his heart were barred in
The blooms of beauty blown,
Yet he who grew the garden
Could call no flower his own.

For by the hands that watered,
The blooms that opened fair
Through frost and pain were scattered
To sweeten the dead air.

A PRAYER

O HOLY SPIRIT of the Hazel, hearken now:
Though shining suns and silver moons burn on the bough,
And though the fruit of stars by many myriads gleam,
Yet in the undergrowth below, still in thy dream,
Lighting the monstrous maze and labyrinthine gloom
Are many gem-winged flowers with gay and delicate bloom.
And in the shade, hearken, O Dreamer of the Tree,
One wild-rose blossom of thy spirit breathed on me
With lovely and still light: a little sister flower
To those that whitely on the tall moon-branches tower.
Lord of the Hazel, now, O hearken while I pray.
This wild-rose blossom of thy spirit fades away.

A LAST COUNSEL

COULD you not in silence borrow
Strength to go from us ungrieving?
All these hours of loving sorrow
Only make more bitter leaving.

You will go forth lonely, thinking
Of the pain you leave behind you;
From the golden sunlight shrinking
For the earthly tears will blind you.

Better, ah, if now we parted
For the little while remaining;
You would seek when broken-hearted
For the mighty heart's sustaining.

You would go then gladly turning
From our place of wounds and weeping,
With your soul for comfort burning
To the mother-bosom creeping.

ORDEAL

LOVE and pity are pleading with me this hour.
  What is this voice that stays me forbidding to yield,
Offering beauty, love, and immortal power,
  Æons away in some far-off heavenly field?

Though I obey thee, Immortal, my heart is sore.
  Though love be withdrawn for love it bitterly grieves:
Pity withheld in the breast makes sorrow more.
  Oh that the heart could feel what the mind believes!

Cease, O love, thy fiery and gentle pleading.
  Soft is thy grief, but in tempest through me it rolls.
Dream'st thou not whither the path is leading
  Where the Dark Immortal would shepherd our weeping souls?

A FAREWELL

ONLY in my deep heart I love you, sweetest heart.
  Many another vesture hath the soul, I pray
Call me not forth from this. If from the light I part
  Only with clay I cling unto the clay.

And ah! my bright companion, you and I must go
  Our ways, unfolding lonely glories, not out own,
Nor from each other gathered, but an inward glow
  Breathed by the Lone One on the seeker lone.

If for the heart's own sake we break the heart, we may
  When the last ruby drop dissolves in diamond light
Meet in a deeper vesture in another day.
  Until that dawn, dear heart, good-night, good-night.

THE VOICE OF THE SEA

THE SEA was hoary, hoary,
Beating on rock and cave:
The winds were white and weeping
With foam dust of the wave.

They thundered louder, louder,
With storm-lips curled in scorn—
And dost thou tremble before us,
O fallen star of morn?

THE HOUR OF TWILIGHT

WHEN the unquiet hours depart
And far away their tumults cease,
Within the twilight of the heart
We bathe in peace, are stilled with peace.

The fire that slew us through the day
For angry deed or sin of sense
Now is the star and homeward ray
To us who bow in penitence.

We kiss the lips of bygone pain
And find a secret sweet in them:
The thorns once dripped with shadowy rain
Are bright upon each diadem.

Ceases the old pathetic strife,
The struggle with the scarlet sin:
The mad enchanted laugh of life
Tempts not the soul that sees within.

No riotous and fairy song
Allures the prodigals who bow
Within the home of law, and throng
Before the mystic Father now,

Where faces of the elder years,
High souls absolved from grief and sin,
Leaning from out ancestral spheres
Beckon the wounded spirit in.

OUR THRONES DECAY

I SAID my pleasure shall not move;
It is not fixed in things apart:
Seeking not love—but yet to love—
I put my trust in mine own heart.

I knew the fountain of the deep
Wells up with living joy, unfed:
Such joys the lonely heart may keep,
And love grow rich with love unwed.

Still flows the ancient fount sublime;—
But, ah, for my heart, shed tears, shed tears;
Not it, but love, has scorn of time,
It turns to dust beneath the years.

RECOLLECTION

THROUGH the blue shadowy valley I hastened in a dream:
Flower rich the night, flower soft the air, a blue flower the stream
I hurried over before I came to the cabin door,
Where the orange flame-glow danced within on the beaten floor.
And the lovely mother who drooped by the sleeping child arose:
And I see how with love her eyes are glad, her face how it glows.
And I know all this was past ten thousand years away,
But in the Ever-Living yesterday is here to-day,
And the beauty made dust we cry out for with so much pain.
Unknown lover, I lived over your joy again.
Long dead maiden, your breasts were warm for the living head.
It is we who have passed from ourselves, from beauty which is not dead.
I know, when I come to my own immortal, I will find there
In a myriad instant all that the wandering soul found fair:
Empires that never crumbled, and thrones all glorious yet,
And hearts ere they were broken, and eyes ere they were wet.

THE WELL OF ALL-HEALING

THERE'S a cure for sorrow in the well at Ballylee
  Where the scarlet cressets hang over the trembling pool:
And joyful winds are blowing from the Land of Youth to me,
  And the heart of the earth is full.

Many and many a sunbright maiden saw the enchanted land
  With star faces glimmer up from the druid wave:
Many and many a pain of love was soothed by a faery hand
  Or lost in the love it gave.

When the quiet with a ring of pearl shall wed the earth,
  And the scarlet berries burn dark by the stars in the pool;
Oh, it's lost and deep I'll be amid the Danaan mirth,
  While the heart of the earth is full.

A NEW THEME

I FAIN would leave the tender songs
  I sang to you of old,
Thinking the oft-sung beauty wrongs
  The magic never told.

And touch no more the thoughts, the moods,
  That win the easy praise;
But venture in the untrodden woods
  To carve the future ways.

Though far or strange or cold appear
  The shadowy things I tell,
Within the heart the hidden seer
  Knows and remembers well.

I think that in the coming time
  The hearts and hopes of men
The mountain tops of life shall climb,
  The gods return again.

I strive to blow the magic horn;
  It feebly murmureth;
Arise on some enchanted morn,
  Poet, with God's own breath!

And sound the horn I cannot blow,
  And by the secret name
Each exile of the heart will know
  Kindle the magic flame.

A DREAM

I WOULD I could weave in
  The colour, the wonder,
The song I conceive in
  My heart while I ponder,

And show how it came like
  The magi of old
Whose chant was a flame like
  The dawn's voice of gold;

Whose dreams followed near them
  A murmur of birds,
And ear still could hear them
  Unchanted in words.

In words I can only
  Reveal thee my heart,
Oh, Light of the Lonely,
  The shining impart.

Between the twilight and the dark
The lights danced up before my eyes:
I found no sleep or peace or rest,
But dreams of stars and burning skies.

I knew the faces of the day—
Dream faces, pale, with cloudy hair,
I knew you not nor yet your home,
The Fount of Shadowy Beauty, where?

I passed a dream of gloomy ways
Where ne'er did human feet intrude:
It was the border of a wood,
A dreadful forest solitude.

With wondrous red and fairy gold
The clouds were woven o'er the ocean;
The stars in fiery æther swung
And danced with gay and glittering motion.

A fire leaped up within my heart
When first I saw the old sea shine;
As if a god were there revealed
I bowed my head in awe divine;

And long beside the dim sea marge
I mused until the gathering haze
Veiled from me where the silver tide
Ran in its thousand shadowy ways.

The black night dropped upon the sea:
The silent awe came down with it:
I saw fantastic vapours flee
As o'er the darkness of the pit.

When lo! from out the furthest night
A speck of rose and silver light
Above a boat shaped wondrously
Came floating swiftly o'er the sea.

It was no human will that bore
The boat so fleetly to the shore
Without a sail spread or an oar.

The Pilot stood erect thereon
And lifted up his ancient face,
Ancient with glad eternal youth
Like one who was of starry race.

His face was rich with dusky bloom;
His eyes a bronze and golden fire;
His hair in streams of silver light
Hung flamelike on his strange attire,

Which, starred with many a mystic sign,
Fell as o'er sunlit ruby glowing:
His light flew o'er the waves afar
In ruddy ripples on each bar
Along the spiral pathways flowing.

It was a crystal boat that chased
The light along the watery waste,
Till caught amid the surges hoary
The Pilot stayed its jewelled glory.

Oh, never such a glory was:
The pale moon shot it through and through
With light of lilac, white and blue:
And there mid many a fairy hue,
Of pearl and pink and amethyst,
Like lightning ran the rainbow gleams
And wove around a wonder-mist.

The Pilot lifted beckoning hands;
Silent I went with deep amaze
To know why came this Beam of Light
So far along the ocean ways
Out of the vast and shadowy night.

"Make haste, make haste!" he cried. "Away!
A thousand ages now are gone.
Yet thou and I ere night be sped
Will reck no more of eve or dawn."

Swift as the swallow to its nest
I leaped: my body dropt right down:
A silver star I rose and flew.
A flame burned golden at his breast:
I entered at the heart and knew
My Brother-Self who roams the deep,
Bird of the wonder-world of sleep.

The ruby vesture wrapped us round
As twain in one; we left behind
The league-long murmur of the shore
And fleeted swifter than the wind.

The distance rushed upon the bark:
We neared unto the mystic isles:
The heavenly city we could mark,
Its mountain light, its jewel dark,
Its pinnacles and starry piles.

The glory brightened: "Do not fear;
For we are real, though what seems
So proudly built above the waves
Is but one mighty spirit's dreams.

"Our Father's house hath many fanes;
Yet enter not and worship not,
For thought but follows after thought
Till last consuming self it wanes.

"The Fount of Shadowy Beauty flings
Its glamour o'er the light of day:
A music in the sunlight sings
To call the dreamy hearts away
Their mighty hopes to ease awhile:
We will not go the way of them:
The chant makes drowsy those who seek
The sceptre and the diadem.

"The Fount of Shadowy Beauty throws
Its magic round us all the night;
What things the heart would be, it sees
And chases them in endless flight.
Or coiled in phantom visions there
It builds within the halls of fire;
Its dreams flash like the peacock's wing
And glow with sun-hues of desire.
We will not follow in their ways
Nor heed the lure of fay or elf,
But in the ending of our days
Rest in the high Ancestral Self."

The boat of crystal touched the shore,
Then melted flamelike from our eyes,
As in the twilight drops the sun
Withdrawing rays of paradise.

We hurried under archéd aisles
That far above in heaven withdrawn
With cloudy pillars stormed the night,
Rich as the opal shafts of dawn.

I would have lingered then—but he:
"Oh, let us haste: the dream grows dim,
Another night, another day,
A thousand years will part from him,
Who is that Ancient One divine
From whom our phantom being born
Rolled with the wonder-light around
Had started in the fairy morn.

"A thousand of our years to him
Are but the night, are but the day,
Wherein he rests from cyclic toil
Or chants the song of starry sway.
He falls asleep: the Shadowy Fount
Fills all our heart with dreams of light:
He wakes to ancient spheres, and we
Through iron ages mourn the night.
We will not wander in the night
But in a darkness more divine
Shall join the Father Light of Lights
And rule the long-descended line."

Even then a vasty twilight fell:
Wavered in air the shadowy towers:
The city like a gleaming shell,
Its azures, opals, silvers, blues,
Were melting in more dreamy hues.
We feared the falling of the night
And hurried more our headlong flight.
In one long line the towers went by;
The trembling radiance dropt behind,
As when some swift and radiant one
Flits by and flings upon the wind
The rainbow tresses of the sun.

And then they vanished from our gaze
Faded the magic lights, and all
Into a starry radiance fell
As waters in their fountain fall.

We knew our time-long journey o'er
And knew the end of all desire,
And saw within the emerald glow
Our Father like the white sun-fire.

We could not say if age or youth
Were on his face: we only burned
To pass the gateways of the day,
The exiles to the heart returned.

He rose to greet us and his breath,
The tempest music of the spheres,
Dissolved the memory of earth,
The cyclic labour and our tears.
In him our dream of sorrow passed,
The spirit once again was free
And heard the song the morning stars
Chant in eternal revelry.

This was the close of human story;
We saw the deep unmeasured shine,
And sank within the mystic glory
They called of old the Dark Divine.

 Well it is gone now,
  The dream that I chanted:
 On this side the dawn now
  I sit fate-implanted.

 But though of my dreaming
  The dawn has bereft me,
 It all was not seeming
  For something has left me.

 I feel in some other
  World far from this cold light
 The Dream Bird, my brother,
  Is rayed with the gold light.

 I too in the Father
  Would hide me, and so,
 Bright Bird, to foregather
  With thee now I go.

THE FEAST OF AGE

SEE where the light streams over Connla's fountain
    Starward aspire!
The sacred sign upon the holy mountain
    Shines in white fire:
Wavering and flaming yonder o'er the snows
    The diamond light
Melts into silver or to sapphire glows,
    Night beyond night:
And from the heaven of heaven descends on earth
    A dew divine.
Come, let us mingle in the starry mirth
    Around the shrine.
O earth, enchantress, mother, to our home
    In thee we press,
Thrilled by thy fiery breath and wrapt in some
    Vast tenderness.
The homeward birds, uncertain o'er their nest
    Wheel in the dome,
Fraught with dim dreams of more enraptured rest,
    Another home.
But gather ye, to whose undarkened eyes
    Night is as day,
Leap forth, immortals, birds of paradise,
    In bright array,
Robed like the shining tresses of the sun,
    And by his name
Call from his haunt divine the ancient one,
    Our father flame.
Aye, from the wonder light, heart of our star,
    Come now, come now.
Sun-breathing spirit, ray thy lights afar:
    Thy children bow,
Hush with more awe the heart; the bright-browed races
    Are nothing worth,
By those dread gods from out whose awful faces
    The earth looks forth
Infinite pity set in calm, whose vision cast
    Adown the years
Beholds how beauty burns away at last
    Their children's tears.

Now while our hearts the ancient quietness
    Floods with its tide,
The things of air and fire and height no less
    In it abide;
And from their wanderings over sea and shore
    They rise as one
Unto the vastness, and with us adore
    The midnight sun,
And enter the innumerable All
    And shine like gold,
And starlike gleam in the immortal's hall,
    The heavenly fold,
And drink the sun-breaths from the mother's lips
    Awhile, and then
Fail from the light and drop in dark eclipse
    To earth again,
Roaming along by heaven-hid promontory
    And valley dim,
Weaving a phantom image of the glory
    They knew in Him.
Out of the fulness flow the winds, their song
    Is heard no more,
Or hardly breathes a mystic sound along
    The dreamy shore,
Blindly they move, unknowing as in trance;
    Their wandering
Is half with us, and half an inner dance,
    Led by the King.

GLORY AND SHADOW

SHADOW

WHO art thou, O Glory,
In flame from the deep
Where stars chant their story;
Why trouble my sleep?
I hardly had rested;
My dreams wither now.
Why comest thou crested
And gemmed on thy brow?

GLORY

Up, Shadow, and follow
The way I will show:
The blue gleaming hollow
To-night we shall know:
And rise through the vast to
The fountain of days
From whence we had passed to
The parting of ways.

SHADOW

I know thee, O Glory;
Thine eyes and thy brow
With white-fire all hoary
Come back to me now.
Together we wandered
In ages agone:
Our thoughts as we pondered
Were stars at the dawn.
My glory has dwindled,
My azure and gold:
Yet you keep unkindled
The sunfire of old.
My footsteps are tied to
The heath and the stone:
My thoughts earth-allied-to,
Ah, leave me alone.

Go back, thou of gladness,
Nor wound me with pain,
Nor smite me with madness,
Nor come nigh again.

GLORY

Why tremble and weep now,
Whom stars once obeyed?
Come forth to the deep now
And be not afraid.
The Dark One is calling
I know, for his dreams
Around me are falling
In musical streams.
A diamond is burning
In depths of the lone,
Thy spirit returning
May claim for its throne.
In flame-fringèd islands
Its sorrow shall cease,
Absorbed in the silence
And quenched in the peace.
Come lay thy poor head on
My heart where it glows
With love ruby-red on
Thy heart for its woes.
My power I surrender;
To thee it is due.
Come forth! for the splendour
Is waiting for you.

THE ROBING OF THE KING

ON the bird of air blue-breasted glint the rays of gold,
And its shadowy fleece above us waves the forest old,
Far through rumorous leagues of midnight stirred by breezes warm.
See the old ascetic yonder, ah, poor withered form,
Where he crouches wrinkled over by unnumbered years
Through the leaves the flakes of moon-fire fall like phantom tears.
At the dawn a kingly hunter swept in proud disdain,
Like a rainbow torrent scattered flashed his royal train.
Now the lonely one unheeded seeks earth's caverns dim:
Never king or prince will robe them radiantly as him
'Mid the deep enfolding darkness follow him, O seer,
Where the arrow will is piercing fiery sphere on sphere,
Through the blackness leaps and sparkles gold and amethyst,
Curling, jetting, and dissolving in a rainbow mist.
In the jewel glow and lunar radiance rises there
One, a morning star in beauty, young, immortal, fair:
Sealed in heavy sleep, the spirit leaves its faded dress,
Unto fiery youth returning out of weariness.
Music as for one departing, joy as for a king,
Sound and swell, and hark! above him cymbals triumphing.
Fire, an aureole encircling, suns his brow with gold,
Like to one who hails the morning on the mountains old.
Open mightier vistas, changing human loves to scorns,
And the spears of glory pierce him like a crown of thorns.
High and yet more high to freedom as a bird he springs,
And the aureole outbreathing, gold and silver wings
Plume the brow and crown the seraph: soon his journey done
He will pass our eyes that follow, sped beyond the sun.
None may know the mystic radiance, King, will there be thine,
Far beyond the light enfolded in the dark divine.

A CALL OF THE SIDHE

TARRY thou yet, late lingerer in the twilight's glory:
Gay are the hills with song: earth's faery children leave
More dim abodes to roam the primrose-hearted eve,
Opening their glimmering lips to breathe some wondrous story.
Hush, not a whisper! Let your heart alone go dreaming.
Dream unto dream may pass: deep in the heart alone
Murmurs the Mighty One his solemn undertone.
Canst thou not see adown the silver cloudland streaming
Rivers of faery light, dewdrop on dewdrop falling,
Star-fire of silver flames, lighting the dark beneath?
And what enraptured hosts burn on the dusky heath!
Come thou away with them for Heaven to Earth is calling.
These are Earth's voice—her answer—spirits thronging.
Come to the Land of Youth: the trees grown heavy there
Drop on the purple wave the starry fruit they bear.
Drink: the immortal waters quench the spirit's longing.
Art thou not now, bright one, all sorrow past, in elation,
Made young with joy, grown brother-hearted with the vast,
Whither thy spirit wending flits the dim stars past
Unto the Light of Lights in burning adoration.

ON A HILLSIDE

A FRIENDLY mountain I know;
As I lie on the green slope there
It sets my heart in a glow
And closes the door on care.

A thought I try to frame—
I was with you long ago;
My soul from your heart out-came;
Mountain, is that not so?

Take me again, dear hills,
Open the door to me
Where the magic murmur thrills
The halls I do not see,

The halls and caverns deep;
Though sometimes I may dare
Down the twilight stairs of sleep
To meet the kingly there.

Sometimes on flaming wings
I sit upon a throne
And watch how the great star swings
Along the sapphire zone.

It has wings of its own for flight,
Diamond its pinions strong,
Glories of opal and white,
I watch the whole night long.

Until I needs must lay
My royal robes aside
To toil in a world of grey,
Grey shadows by my side.

And when I ponder it o'er
Grey memories only bide,
But their fading lips tell more
Than all the world beside.

A RETURN

WE turned back mad from the mystic mountains,
All foamed with red and with elfin gold:
Up from the heart of the twilight's fountains
The fires enchanted were starward rolled.

We turned back mad: we thought of the morrow,
The iron clang of the far-away town:
We could not weep in our bitter sorrow,
But joy as an Arctic sun went down.

THE CHILD OF DESTINY

THIS is the hero-heart of the enchanted isle,
Whom now the twilight children tenderly enfold,
Pat with their pearly palms and crown with elfin gold,
While in the mountain's breast his brothers watch and smile.
Who now of Dana's host may guide these dancing feet?
What bright immortal hides and through a child's light breath
Laughs an immortal joy—Angus of love and death
Returned to make our hearts with dream and music beat?
Or Lu leaves heavenly wars to free his ancient land;
Not on the fiery steed maned with tumultuous flame
As in the Fomor days the sunbright chieftain came,
But in this dreaming boy, more subtle conquest planned.
Or does the Mother brood some deed of sacrifice?
Her heart in his laid bare to hosts of wounding spears,
Till love immortal melt the cruel eyes to tears,
Or on his brow be set the heroes' thorny prize.
See! as some shadows of a darker race draw near,
How he compels their feet, with what a proud command!
What is it waves and gleams? Is that a Silver Hand
Whose light through delicate lifted fingers shines so clear?
Night like a glowing seraph o'er the kingly boy
Watches with ardent eyes from his own ancient home;
And far away, rocking in living foam
The three great waves leap up exulting in their joy,
Remembering the past, the immemorial deeds
The Danaan gods had wrought in guise of mortal men,
Their elemental hearts madden with life again,
And shaking foamy heads toss the great ocean steeds.

MAGIC

After Reading the Upanishads

OUT of the dusky chamber of the brain
Flows the imperial will through dream on dream:
The fires of life around it tempt and gleam;
The lights of earth behind it fade and wane.

Passed beyond beauty tempting dream on dream,
The pure will seeks the heart-hold of the light:
Sounds the deep OM, the mystic word of might:
Forth from the heart-hold breaks the living stream.

Passed out beyond the deep heart music-filled,
The kingly will sits on the ancient throne,
Wielding the sceptre, fearless, free, alone,
Knowing in Brahma all it dared and willed.

BREAGHY

WHEN twilight flutters the mountains over,
The faery lights from the earth unfold:
And over the caves enchanted hover
The giant heroes and gods of old.
The bird of æther its flaming pinions
Waves over earth the whole night long:
The stars drop down in their blue dominions
To hymn together their choral song.
The child of earth in his heart grows burning,
Mad for the night and the deep unknown;
His alien flame in a dream returning
Seats itself on the ancient throne.
When twilight over the mountains fluttered,
And night with its starry millions came,
I too had dreams: the songs I have uttered
Come from this heart that was touched by the flame.

A FAREWELL

I GO down from the hills half in gladness, and half with a pain I depart,
Where the Mother with gentlest breathing made music on lip and in
     heart;
For I know that my childhood is over: a call comes out of the vast,
And the love that I had in the old time, like beauty in twilight, is past.

I am fired by a Danaan whisper of battles afar in the world,
And my thought is no longer of peace, for the banners in dream are
     unfurled,
And I pass from the council of stars and of hills to a life that is new:
And I bid to you stars and you mountains a tremulous long adieu.

I will come once again as a master, who played here as child in my dawn
I will enter the heart of the hills where the gods of the old world are gone.
And will war like the bright Hound of Ulla with princes of earth and
     of sky.
For my dream is to conquer the heavens and battle for kingship on high.

ON BEHALF OF SOME IRISHMEN NOT FOLLOWERS OF TRADITION

THEY call us aliens, we are told,
Because our wayward visions stray
From that dim banner they unfold,
The dreams of worn-out yesterday.
The sum of all the past is theirs,
The creeds, the deeds, the fame, the name,
Whose death-created glory flares
And dims the spark of living flame.
They weave the necromancer's spell,
And burst the graves where martyrs slept,
Their ancient story to retell,
Renewing tears the dead have wept.
And they would have us join their dirge,
This worship of an extinct fire
In which they drift beyond the verge
Where races all outworn expire.
The worship of the dead is not
A worship that our hearts allow,
Though every famous shade were wrought
With woven thorns above the brow.
We fling our answer back in scorn:
"We are less children of this clime
Than of some nation yet unborn
Or empire in the womb of time.
We hold the Ireland in the heart
More than the land our eyes have seen,
And love the goal for which we start
More than the tale of what has been."
The generations as they rise
May live the life men lived before,
Still hold the thought once held as wise,
Go in and out by the same door.
We leave the easy peace it brings:
The few we are shall still unite
In fealty to unseen kings
Or unimaginable light.
We would no Irish sign efface,

But yet our lips would gladlier hail
The firstborn of the Coming Race
Than the last splendour of the Gael.
No blazoned banner we unfold—
One charge alone we give to youth,
Against the sceptred myth to hold
The golden heresy of truth.

AN IRISH FACE

NOT her own sorrow only that hath place
Upon yon gentle face.
Too slight have been her childhood's years to gain
The imprint of such pain.
It hid behind her laughing hours, and wrought
Each curve in saddest thought
On brow and lips and eyes. With subtle art
It made that little heart
Through its young joyous beatings to prepare
A quiet shelter there,
Where the immortal sorrows might find a home.
And many there have come;
Bowed in a mournful mist of golden hair
Deirdre hath entered there.
And shrouded in a fall of pitying dew,
Weeping the friend he slew,
The Hound of Ulla lies, with those who shed
Tears for the Wild Geese fled.
And all the lovers on whom fate had warred
Cutting the silver cord
Enter, and softly breath by breath they mould
The young heart to the old,
The old protest, the old pity, whose power
Are gathering to the hour
When their knit silence shall be mightier far
Than leagued empires are.
And dreaming of the sorrow on this face
We grow of lordlier race,
Could shake the rooted rampart of the hills
To shield her from all ills,
And through a deep adoring pity won
Grow what we dream upon.

IN CONNEMARA

WITH eyes all untroubled she laughs as she passes,
  Bending beneath the creel with the seaweed brown,
Till evening with pearl dew dims the shining grasses
  And night lit with dreamlight enfolds the sleepy town.

Then she will wander, her heart all a laughter,
  Tracking the dream star that lights the purple gloom.
She follows the proud and golden races after,
  As high as theirs her spirit, as high will be her doom.

TWILIGHT BY THE CABIN

DUSK, a pearl-grey river, o'er
  Hill and vale puts out the day—
What do you wonder at, asthore,
  What's away in yonder grey?

Dark the eyes that linger long—
  Dream-fed heart, awake, come in,
Warm the hearth and gay the song:
  Love with tender words would win.

Fades the eve in dreamy fire,
  But the heart of night is lit:
Ancient beauty, old desire,
  By the cabin doorway flit.

This is Etain's land and line,
  And the homespun cannot hide
Kinship with a race divine,
  Thrill of rapture, light of pride.

There her golden kinsmen are:
  And her heart a moment knew
Angus like the evening star
  Fleeting through the dusk and dew.

Throw the woman's mask away:
  Wear the opal glimmering dress;
Let the feathered starlight ray
  Over every gleaming tress.

Child of Etain, wherefore leave
  Light and laughter, joyful years,
For the earth's grey coloured eve
  Ever dropping down with tears?

Was it for some love of old?
  Ah, reveal thyself. The bars
On the gateway would not hold:
  He will follow to the stars.

KINSHIP

IN summer time, with high imaginings
Of proud Crusaders and of Paynim kings,
The children crowned themselves with famous names,
And fought there, building up their merry games,
Their mimic war, from old majestic things.

There was no bitter hate then in the fight,
For ancient law ruled victory and flight,
And, victory and defeat alike forgot,
They slept together in the selfsame cot,
With arms about each other through the night.

Ah, did our greatest on the battle-field
See such a love, all magical, revealed,
Pausing in combat? did they recognise
Kinships in Tirnanoge through flashing eyes,
What lovely brotherhood the foe concealed?

And did they know, when all fierce wars were done,
To what high home or dun their feet would run?
What outstretched love would meet them at the gate?
And that the end of the long road of hate
Was adoration when the goal was won?

Could you and I but of each other say
From what a lordly House we took our way,
And to what Hostel of the Gods we wend,
Oh would we not anticipate the end?
Oh would we not have paradise to-day?

THE JOY OF EARTH

OH, the sudden wings arising from the ploughed fields brown
  Showered aloft in spray of song the wild-bird twitter floats
O'er the unseen fount awhile, and then comes dropping down
  Nigh the cool brown earth to hush enraptured notes.

Far within a dome of trembling opal throbs the fire,
  Mistily its rain of diamond lances shed below
Touches eyes and brows and faces lit with wild desire
  For the burning silence whither we would go.

Heart, be young; once more it is the ancient joy of earth
  Breathes in thee and flings the wild wings sunward to the dome
To the light where all the children of the fire had birth
  Though our hearts and footsteps wander far from home.

THE IRON AGE

HOW came this pigmy rabble spun,
After the gods and kings of old,
Upon a tapestry begun
With threads of silver and of gold?
In heaven began the heroic tale
What meaner destinies prevail!

They wove about the antique brow
A circlet of the heavenly air.
To whom is due such reverence now,
The thought "What deity is there"?
We choose the chieftains of our race
From hucksters in the market place.

When in their councils over all
Men set the power that sells and buys,
Be sure the price of life will fall,
Death be more precious in our eyes.
Have all the gods their cycles run?
Has devil worship now begun?

O whether devil planned or no,
Life here is ambushed, this our fate,
That road to anarchy doth go,
This to the grim mechanic state.
The gates of hell are open wide,
But lead to other hells outside.

How has the fire Promethean paled?
Who is there now who wills or dares
Follow the fearless chiefs who sailed,
Celestial adventurers,
Who charted in undreamt of skies
The magic zones of paradise?

Mankind that sought to be god-kind,
To wield the sceptre, wear the crown,
What made it wormlike in its mind?
Who bade it lay the sceptre down?
Was it through any speech of thee,
Misunderstood of Galilee?

The whip was cracked in Babylon
That slaves unto the gods might raise
The golden turrets nigh the sun.
Yet beggars from the dust might gaze
Upon the mighty builders' art
And be of proud uplifted heart.

We now are servile to the mean
Who once were slaves unto the proud.
No lordlier life on earth has been
Although the heart be lowlier bowed.
Is there an iron age to be
With beauty but a memory?

Send forth, who promised long ago,
"I will not leave thee or forsake,"
Someone to whom our hearts may flow
With adoration, though we make
The crucifixion be the sign,
The meed of all the kingly line.

The morning stars were heard to sing
When man towered golden in the prime.
One equal memory let us bring
Before we face our night in time.
Grant us one only evening star,
The iron age's avatar.

AGE AND YOUTH

WE have left our youth behind:
  Earth is in its baby years:
Void of wisdom cries the wind,
  And the sunlight knows no tears.

When shall twilight feel the awe,
  All the rapt thought of the sage,
And the lips of wind give law
  Drawn from out their lore of age?

When shall earth begin to burn
  With such love as thrills my breast?
When shall we together turn
  To our long, long home for rest?

Child and father, we grow old
  While you laugh and play with flowers;
And life's tale for us is told
  Holding only empty hours.

Giant child, on you await
  All the hopes and fears of men.
In thy fulness is our fate—
  What till then, oh, what till then?

THE PARTING OF WAYS

THE SKIES from black to pearly grey
  Had veered without a star or sun;
Only a burning opal ray
  Fell on your brow when all was done.

Aye, after victory, the crown;
  Yet through the fight no word of cheer;
And what would win and what go down
  No word could help, no light make clear.

A thousand ages onward led
  Their joys and sorrows to that hour;
No wisdom weighed, no word was said,
  For only what we were had power.

There was no tender leaning there
  Of brow to brow in loving mood;
For we were rapt apart, and were
  In elemental solitude.

We knew not in redeeming day
  whether our spirits would be found
Floating along the starry way,
  Or in the earthly vapours drowned.

Brought by the sunrise-coloured flame
  To earth, uncertain yet, the while
I looked at you, there slowly came,
  Noble and sisterly, your smile.

We bade adieu to love the old;
  We heard another lover then,
Whose forms are myriad and untold,
  Sigh to us from the hearts of men.

HOPE IN FAILURE

THOUGH now thou hast failed and art fallen, despair not because of
    defeat,
Though lost for a while be thy heaven and weary of earth be thy feet,
For all will be beauty about thee hereafter through sorrowful years,
And lovely the dews for thy chilling and ruby thy heart-drip of tears.

The eyes that had gazed from afar on a beauty that blinded the eyes
Shall call forth its image for ever, its shadow in alien skies.
The heart that had striven to beat in the heart of the Mighty too soon
Shall still of that beating remember some errant and faltering tune.

For thou hast but fallen to gather the last of the secrets of power;
The beauty that breathes in thy spirit shall shape of thy sorrow a flower,
The pale bud of pity shall open the bloom of its tenderest rays,
The heart of whose shining is bright with the light of the Ancient of Days.

FAITH

HERE where the loves of others close
The vision of my heart begins.
The wisdom that within us grows
Is absolution for our sins.

We took forbidden fruit and ate
Far in the garden of His mind.
The ancient prophecies of hate
We proved untrue, for He was kind.

He does not love the bended knees,
The soul made wormlike in His sight,
Within whose heaven are hierarchies
And solar kings and lords of light.

Who come before Him with the pride
The Children of the King should bear,
They will not be by Him denied,
His light will make their darkness fair.

To be afar from Him is death
Yet all things find their fount in Him:
And nearing to the sunrise breath
Shine jewelled like the seraphim.

A MIDNIGHT MEDITATION

HOW often have I said,
"We may not grieve for the immortal dead."
And now, poor blenchèd heart,
Thy ruddy hues all tremulous depart.
Why be with fate at strife
Because one passes on from death to life,
Who may no more delay
Rapt from our strange and pitiful dream away
By one with ancient claim
Who robes her with the spirit like a flame.
Not lost this high belief—
Oh, passionate heart, what is thy cause for grief?
Is this thy sorrow now,
She in eternal beauty may not bow
Thy troubles to efface
As in old time a head with gentle grace
All tenderly laid by thine
Taught thee the nearness of the love divine.
Her joys no more for thee
Than the impartial laughter of the sea,
Her beauty no more fair
For thee alone, but starry, everywhere.
Her pity dropped for you
No more than heaven above with healing dew
Favours one home of men—
Ah! grieve not; she becomes herself again,
And passed beyond thy sight
She roams along the thought-swept fields of light,
Moving in dreams until
She finds again the root of ancient will,
The old heroic love
That emptied once the heavenly courts above.
The angels heard from earth
A mournful cry which shattered all their mirth,
Raised by a senseless rout
Warring in chaos with discordant shout,
And that the pain might cease
They grew rebellious in the Master's peace;
And falling downward then
The angelic lights were crucified in men;

Leaving so radiant spheres
For earth's dim twilight ever wet with tears
That through those shadows dim
Might breathe the lovely music brought from Him.
And now my grief I see
Was but that ancient shadow part of me,
Not yet attuned to good,
Still blind and senseless in its warring mood,
I turn from it and climb
To the heroic spirit of the prime,
The light that well foreknew
All the dark ways that it must journey through.
Yet seeing still a gain,
A distant glory o'er the hills of pain,
Through all that chaos wild
A breath as gentle as a little child,
Through earth transformed, divine,
The Christ-soul of the universe to shine.

ENDURANCE

HE bent above: so still her breath
What air she breathed he could not say,
Whether in worlds of life or death:
So softly ebbed away, away,
The life that had been light to him,
So fled her beauty leaving dim
The emptying chambers of his heart
Thrilled only by the pang and smart,
The dull and throbbing agony
That suffers still, yet knows not why.
Love's immortality so blind
Dreams that all things with it conjoined
Must share with it immortal day:
But not of this—but not of this—
The touch, the eyes, the laugh, the kiss,
Fall from it and it goes its way.
So blind he wept above her clay,
"I did not think that you could die.
Only some veil would cover you
Our loving eyes could still pierce through;
And see through dusky shadows still
Move as of old your wild sweet will,
Impatient every heart to win
And flash its heavenly radiance in."
Though all the worlds were sunk in rest
The ruddy star within his breast
Would croon its tale of ancient pain,
Its sorrow that would never wane,
Its memory of the days of yore
Moulded in beauty evermore.
Ah, immortality so blind,
To dream all things with it conjoined
Must follow it from star to star
And share with it immortal years.
The memory, yearning, grief, and tears,
Fall from it and it goes afar.
He walked at night along the sands,
He saw the stars dance overhead,
He had no memory of the dead,
But lifted up exultant hands

To hail the future like a boy,
The myriad paths his feet might press.
Unhaunted by old tenderness
He felt an inner secret joy—
A spirit of unfettered will
Through light and darkness moving still
Within the All to find its own,
To be immortal and alone.

DESTINY

LIKE winds or waters were her ways:
The flowing tides, the airy streams,
Are troubled not by any dreams;
They know the circle of their days.

Like winds or waters were her ways:
They heed not immemorial cries;
They move to their high destinies
Beyond the little voice that prays.

She passed into her secret goal,
And left behind a soul that trod
In darkness, knowing not of God,
But craving for its sister soul.

WHEN

WHEN mine hour is come
Let no teardrop fall
And no darkness hover
Round me where I lie.
Let the vastness call
One who was its lover,
Let me breathe the sky.

Where the lordly light
Walks along the world,
And its silent tread
Leaves the grasses bright,
Leaves the flowers uncurled,
Let me to the dead
Breathe a gay goodnight.

TRANSFORMATIONS

WHAT miracle was it that made this grey Rathgar
Seem holy earth, a leaping-place from star to star?
I know I strode along grey streets disconsolate,
Seeing nowhere a glimmer of the Glittering Gate,
My vision baffled amid many dreams, for still
The airy walls rose up in fabulous hill on hill.
The stars were fortresses upon the dizzy slope
And one and all were unassailable by hope.
And then I turned and looked beyond high Terenure
Where the last jewel breath of twilight floated pure,
As if god Angus there, with his enchanted lyre,
Sat swaying his bright body and hair of misty fire,
And smote the slumber-string within the heavenly house
That eve might lay upon the earth her tender brows,
Her moth-dim tresses, and lip's invisible bloom,
And eye's light shadowed under eyelids of the gloom,
Till all that dark divine pure being, breast to breast,
Lay cool upon the sleepy isle from east to west.
Then I took thought remembering many a famous tale
Told of those heavenly adventurers the Gael,
Ere to a far-brought alien worship they inclined,
And that its sorceries had left them shorn and blind,
Crownless and sceptreless, while yet their magic might
Could bow the lordly pillars of the day and night,
And topple in one golden wreckage stars and sun,
And mix their precious fires till heaven and earth were one.
Then god and hero mingled, and the veil was rent
That hid the fairy turrets in the firmament,
The lofty god-uplifted cities that flash on high
Dense with the silver-radiant deities of sky,
And the gay populace that under ocean bide
Unknowing of the flowing of the ponderous tide,
And worlds where Time is full, where all with one accord
Turn the flushed beauty of their faces to the Lord,
Where the last ecstasy lights up each hill and glade
And love is not remembered between man and maid,
For lips laugh there at beauty the heart imagineth,
And feet dance there at the holy Bridal of Love and Death.
And as, with heart upborne and speedier footsteps, I
Strode on my way, that twilight-burnished sky

Seemed to heave up as from a mystic fountain thrown.
And world on world those magic voyagers had known
Glowed in the vast with burning hill and glittering stream,
And all their shining folk, till earth was as a dream,
A memory fleeting moth-like in the light to be
Scorched by the fiery Dreamer of Eternity.
And the bright host swept by me like a blazing wind
O'er the dark churches where the blind mislead the blind.

TRAGEDY

A MAN went forth one day at eve:
The long day's toil for him was done:
The eye that scanned the page could leave
Its task until tomorrow's sun.

Upon the threshold where he stood
Flared on his tired eyes the sight,
Where host on host the multitude
Burned fiercely in the dusky night.

The starry lights at play—at play—
The giant children of the blue,
Heaped scorn upon his trembling clay
And with their laughter pierced him through.

They seemed to say in scorn of him
"The power we have was once in thee.
King, is thy spirit grown so dim,
That thou art slave and we are free?"

As out of him the power—the power—
The free—the fearless, whirled in play,
He knew himself that bitter hour
The close of all his royal day.

And from the stars' exultant dance
Within the fiery furnace glow,
Exile of all the vast expanse,
He turned him homeward sick and slow.

THE EVERLASTING BATTLE

WHEN in my shadowy hours I pierce the hidden heart of hopes and fears,
They change into immortal joys or end in immemorial tears.
Moytura's battle still endures and in this human heart of mine
The golden sun powers with the might of demon darkness intertwine.

I think that every teardrop shed still flows from Balor's eye of doom,
And gazing on his ageless grief my heart is filled with ageless gloom:
I close my ever-weary eyes and in my bitter spirit brood
And am at one in vast despair with all the demon multitude.

But in the lightning flash of hope I feel the sungod's fiery sling
Has smote the horror in the heart where clouds of demon glooms
        take wing,
I shake my heavy fears aside and seize the flaming sword of will,
I am of Dana's race divine and know I am immortal still.

IN MEMORIAM

POOR little child, my pretty boy,
Why did the hunter mark thee out?
Wert thou betrayed by thine own joy?
Singled through childhood's merry shout?

And who on such a gentle thing
Let slip the Hound that none may bar,
That shall o'ertake the swiftest wing
And tear the heavens down star by star?

And borne away unto the night,
What comfort in the vasty hall?
Can That which towers from depth to height
Melt in Its mood majestical,

And laugh with thee as child to child?
Or shall the gay light in thine eyes
Drop stricken there before the piled
Immutable immensities?

Or shall the Heavenly Wizard turn
Thy frailty to might in Him,
And make my laughing elf to burn
Comrade of crested cherubim?

The obscure vale emits no sound,
No sight, the chase has hurried far:
The Quarry and the phantom Hound,
Where are they now? Beyond what star?

MOMENTARY

THE SWEETEST song was ever sung
  May soothe you but a little while:
The gayest music ever rung
  Shall yield you but a fleeting smile.

The well I digged you soon shall pass:
  You may but rest with me an hour:
Yet drink, I offer you the glass,
  A moment of sustaining power,

And give to you, if it be gain,
  Whether in pleasure or annoy,
To see one elemental pain,
  One light of everlasting joy.

UNITY

ONE thing in all things have I seen:
One thought has haunted earth and air:
Clangour and silence both have been
Its palace chambers. Everywhere

I saw the mystic vision flow
And live in men and woods and streams,
Until I could no longer know
The dream of life from my own dreams.

Sometimes it rose like fire in me
Within the depths of my own mind,
And spreading to infinity,
It took the voices of the wind:

It scrawled the human mystery—
Dim heraldry—on light and air;
Wavering along the starry sea
I saw the flying vision there.

Each fire that in God's temple lit
Burns fierce before the inner shrine,
Dimmed as my fire grew near to it
And darkened at the light of mine.

At last, at last, the meaning caught—
The spirit wears its diadem;
It shakes its wondrous plumes of thought
And trails the stars along with them.

CONTENT

WHO are exiles? As for me
Where beneath the diamond dome
Lies the light on hill or tree,
There my palace is and home.

Who are lonely lacking care?
Here the winds are living, press
Close on bosom, lips and hair—
Well I know their soft caress.

Sad or fain no more to live?
I have pressed the lips of pain;
With the kisses lovers give,
Ransomed ancient joys again.

Captive? See what stars give light
In the hidden heart of clay:
At their radiance dark and bright
Fades the dreamy king of day.

Night and day no more eclipse
Friendly eyes that on us shine,
Speech from old familiar lips
Playmates of a youth divine.

Come away, O, come away;
We will quench the heart's desire
Past the gateways of the day
In the rapture of the fire.

RECONCILIATION

I BEGIN through the grass once again to be bound to the Lord;
  I can see, through a face that has faded, the face full of rest
Of the earth, of the mother, my heart with her heart in accord,
  As I lie 'mid the cool green tresses that mantle her breast
I begin with the grass once again to be bound to the Lord.

By the hand of a child I am led to the throne of the King
  For a touch that now fevers me not is forgotten and far,
And His infinite sceptred hands that sway us can bring
  Me in dreams from the laugh of a child to the song of a star.
On the laugh of a child I am borne to the joy of the King.

EPILOGUE

WELL, when all is said and done
Best within my narrow way,
May some angel of the sun
Muse memorial o'er my clay:

"Here was beauty all betrayed
From the freedom of her state;
From her human uses stayed
On an idle rhyme to wait.

"Ah, what deep despair might move
If the beauty lit a smile,
Or the heart was warm with love
That was pondering the while.

"He has built his monument
With the winds of time at strife,
Who could have before he went
Written on the book of life.

"To the stars from which he came
Empty handed, he goes home;
He who might have wrought in flame
Only traced upon the foam."

NOTE ON CELTIC
MYTHOLOGICAL ALLUSIONS

AS the mythological references made in a few poems may partially obscure the meaning for those unacquainted with Celtic tradition, I have appended here a brief commentary on the names mentioned.

Angus, the Celtic Eros. In the bardic stories he is described as a tall, golden-haired youth playing on a harp and surrounded by singing birds. The kisses of these birds brought love and after that death.

Balor, the prince of the dark powers. His eye turned every living thing it rested on into stone. He was killed at the battle of Moytura by Lu the Sun-god.

Dana, the Hibernian mother of the gods who were named from her Tuatha De Danaan, or the Tribes of the goddess Dana. They are also sometimes called the Sidhe.

Etain, a Celtic goddess who is the subject of a famous story, "The Wooing of Etain." She left the heaven world and became the wife of an ancient Irish king.

Lir, the Oceanus of Celtic mythology. Probably the Great Deep or original divinity from whom all sprang. His son Mananan MacLir was the most spiritual divinity known to the ancient Gael. Lir is more familiar as the father of the children who were changed into swans by magic, and who lived for long ages on the waters around the Irish coast. The story of the fate of the children of Lir was probably in its earliest form a mythological account of the descent of the spirit from the Heaven-world to the Earth and its final redemption.

Lu or *Lugh*, the great god of light who led the De Danaans at the battle of Moytura, and who slew Balor of the Evil Eye by a cast from his sling. He is a Celtic Hermes or Apollo.

Fomor, the dark powers who were opposed to the hosts of light, the Tuatha De Danaan. They enslaved the latter for a time until the De Danaans rose, led by Lu the Sun-god, and defeated the Fomors in the battle of Moytura.

Silver Hand. Nuada, one of the Danaan divinities, is called Nuada of the Silver Hand.

Hound of Ulla. Cuculain, the great champion of the Red Branch cycle of tales.

Sacred Hazel, the Celtic tree of life. It grew over Connla's Well, and the fruit which fell from it were the Nuts of Knowledge which give wisdom and inspiration. Connla's Well is a Celtic equivalent of the First Fountain of mysticism. As an old story states, "The folk of many arts have all drunk from that fountain."

"The three great waves" are "the wave of Toth, the wave of Rury, and the long, slow, white-foaming wave of Cluna." In the bardic stories these three mystical waves shout round the coast of Ireland in recognition of great kings and heroes.

"The Feast of Age," the druidic form of the mysteries. It was instituted by Mananan MacLir, and whoever partook of the feast became immortal.